Pizza

GENERAL EDITOR
CHUCK WILLIAMS

RECIPES
LORENZA DE' MEDICI

PHOTOGRAPHY
ALLAN ROSENBERG

TIME
LIFE
BOOKS

TIME-LIFE BOOKS
Time-Life Books is a division of Time Life Inc.
Time-Life is a trademark of Time Warner Inc. U.S.A.

Time-Life Custom Publishing
Vice President and Publisher: Terry Newell
Director of New Product Development: Regina Hall
Managing Editor: Donia Ann Steele
Director of Sales: Neil Levin
Director of Financial Operations: J. Brian Birky

WILLIAMS-SONOMA
Founder/Vice-Chairman: Chuck Williams

WELDON OWEN INC.
President: John Owen
Publisher: Wendely Harvey
Managing Editor: Laurie Wertz
Consulting Editor: Norman Kolpas
Copy Editor: Sharon Silva
Recipe Translation: Michael and Anthony Dunkley
Design/Editorial Assistant: Janique Poncelet
Design: John Bull, The Book Design Company
Production: Stephanie Sherman, James Obata,
    Mick Bagnato
Production Coordinator: Tarji Mickelson
Co-Editions Director: Derek Barton
Food Photographer: Allan Rosenberg
Additional Food Photography: Allen V. Lott
Primary Food & Prop Stylist: Sandra Griswold
Food Stylist: Heidi Gintner
Assistant Food Stylist: Danielle Di Salvo
Prop Assistant: Karen Nicks
Glossary Illustrations: Alice Harth

The Williams-Sonoma Kitchen Library
conceived and produced by Weldon Owen Inc.
814 Montgomery St., San Francisco, CA 94133

In collaboration with Williams-Sonoma
3250 Van Ness Ave., San Francisco, CA 94109

Production by Mandarin Offset, Hong Kong
Printed in China

A Note on Weights and Measures:
All recipes include customary U.S. and metric
measurements. Metric conversions are based on
a standard developed for these books and have
been rounded off. Actual weights may vary.

A Weldon Owen Production

Copyright © 1993 Weldon Owen Inc.
Reprinted in 1993; 1993; 1993; 1993; 1994; 1995; 1995;
1996; 1996; 1996

Library of Congress
Cataloging-in-Publication Data:

De' Medici Stucchi, Lorenza, 1926-
    Pizza / general editor, Chuck Williams ;
recipes, Lorenza de' Medici ; photography,
Allan Rosenberg.
        p.   cm. — (Williams-Sonoma kitchen library)
    Includes index.
    ISBN 0-7835-0229-X (trade) ;
    ISBN 0-7835-0230-3 (LSB)
    1. Pizza. I. Williams, Chuck.
II. Title.   III. Series.
TX770.P58D43   1993
641.8'24—dc20   92-27838
                                                         CIP

Contents

CHEESE, VEGETABLE & HERB PIZZAS 17

MEAT & SEAFOOD PIZZAS 57

FRUIT PIZZAS 69

CALZONE 85

INTRODUCTION

The first pizzas were no doubt products as much of frugality as of creativity. An Italian home cook, finding some extra bread dough on hand, flattened it, spread on some leftover pasta sauce, added a few parings of cheese and popped it in the oven.

Today, pizza has evolved into one of the foods we are most likely to eat when we dine out or order in. But it still has about it that air of homespun improvisation. This book's goal is to bring pizza making into the home kitchen, where it rightly belongs.

On the next few pages, you'll find everything you need to know to make a pizza with absolute ease in your own home, from a survey of equipment to step-by-step demonstrations of preparing the dough and shaping and baking the pizza. These basics will enable you to make any of the 44 recipes that follow for both savory pizzas and sweet dessert pizzas, as well as calzone, their turnover-style cousins.

I think you'll be impressed by how easy pizza making is. The dough, for example, is quickly mixed and kneaded, and requires just an hour or two to rise. If you cannot wait that long, substitute a simple baking-powder dough, or even a store-bought pizza dough.

I'm sure you'll also be surprised by the incredible variety this book displays. You can make pizza in all manner of shapes and sizes, from bite-sized hors d'oeuvres to large circles, rectangular pan pizzas to calzone plump with fillings. You can moisten a pizza with any number of sauces—or use no sauce at all—and top it with meats, poultry, seafood, cheeses, vegetables, or fresh or dried herbs. And you can even make pizza for dessert by simply topping a quick baking powder–leavened dough with fresh or dried fruits.

The possibilities are nearly countless—a far cry, indeed, from that frugal Italian cook's first hasty creation.

EQUIPMENT

Basic and specialized tools and accessories
for making professional-quality pizzas

A few widely available pieces of equipment can help you achieve results equal to those of any pizzeria.

Basic kitchen tools—from knives to measuring cups, bowls to graters—are used to prepare doughs, sauces and toppings. And if you do not already have a good oven thermometer, you may want to get one to make sure your pizza bakes at the correct temperature.

Most notable among the more specialized equipment shown here is a pizza stone or baking tiles—the preferred surface upon which to bake pizzas. Thoroughly preheated, they reproduce the intense, dry, radiant heat of a professional baker's oven, resulting in crisp, well-browned crusts.

1. Baking Stone
Made of the same clay that lines commercial pottery kilns, this porous stone absorbs moisture, producing a dry heat that crisps crusts. Preheat on the bottom of the oven or on the lowest rack. Available in circular and rectangular shapes, large and smaller sizes.

2. Pizza Serving Pan
Restaurant-style metal pan, preferably aluminum, to which baked pizza is transferred for cutting and serving.

3. Liquid Measuring Cup
Accurately measures liquid ingredients. Choose heavy-duty, heat-resistant glass, marked on one side in cups and ounces; on the other in milliliters. Lip and handle ensure easy pouring.

4. Oil Can
Protects oil from exposure to light and air. Long spout is good for drizzling oil over pizza.

5. Basting Brush
Evenly spreads sauces or oil over pizza dough. Choose a small, sturdy brush with well-attached natural bristles.

6. Pizza Server
Sturdy server with wedge-shaped blade, for serving individual slices of round pizzas.

7. Paring Knife
For cutting up small topping ingredients.

8. Baking Sheet
Stick-resistant sheet, rimless on two sides, conveniently holds

miniature pizzas for baking. May also be used in place of a peel for transferring pizzas to and from the oven.

9. Pizza Baking Pan
Neatly holds pizzas with maximum toppings, which might fall apart if slid directly from peel to baking stone. Stick-resistant coating facilitates serving and cleanup. Choose heavy-gauge metal to prevent warping in intense oven heat.

10. Crisping Pan
Perforations in metal pan allow hot air to pass through, crisping leftover pizza during brief reheating. May also be used as a baking pan for freshly made pizzas.

11. Four-Sided Shredder/Slicer
Standard, sturdy stainless-steel model for shredding, grating and slicing cheese toppings.

12. Dowel-Type Rolling Pin
For rolling out pizza dough on a work surface. Select a sturdy hardwood pin, at least 12 inches (30 cm) long. To prevent warping, do not wash; wipe clean with a dry cloth.

13. Dry Measuring Cups
In graduated sizes, for measuring dry ingredients for dough. Straight rims allow ingredients to be leveled accurately.

14. Measuring Spoons
In graduated sizes, for measuring small quantities of ingredients such as yeast and salt. Choose good-quality, calibrated metal spoons with deep bowls.

15. Baking Tiles
High-fired terra-cotta tiles produce intense, dry oven heat for crisp, well-browned pizzas. Metal tray neatly holds tiles. Preheat on the bottom of the oven or on the lowest rack.

16. Pizza Screen
Pizzas with ample toppings may be shaped and baked directly on top of fine stainless-steel mesh, for easy transfer to and from the oven.

17. Baker's Peel
Smooth-surfaced wood or metal paddle upon which pizzas can be shaped and topped for sliding directly into the oven. Beveled edge helps the peel to slide easily under a finished pizza to retrieve it from the oven.

18. Flat Grater
For grating hard cheeses to top pizzas.

19. Dough Scraper
Useful for lifting pizza dough and for cleaning work surfaces after dough is made. Choose a sturdy stainless-steel scraper with a metal or wood handle.

20. Oven Thermometer
Provides accurate reading of oven temperature. May be stood directly on top of the baking stone or tiles, to check that the surface has reached desired preheated temperature before pizza is baked.

21. Mixing Bowl
For mixing pizza dough and leaving it to rise.

22. Cutting Wheel
Cuts pizzas into individual slices. Choose a sturdy model with a well-attached handle and a sharp, good-sized wheel.

23. Crock of Pizza Herbs
Earthenware crock holds blend of fine-textured, dried herbs close at hand for seasoning pizza toppings.

24. Straight-Sided Spatula
For transferring small or unusual-shaped pizzas to or from baking surfaces, and for serving individual square or rectangular pizza slices.

MAKING PIZZA DOUGH

Simple steps for a perfect crust every time

No part of a pizza divides opinion more among pizza lovers than the crust, with preferences ranging from thin and crisp to thick and breadlike.

The key to success, in truth, is not found in one secret recipe, but rather in a repertoire of different doughs, each good in its own right. The dough recipes on the following pages are virtually interchangeable, although each is best suited to certain sauces and toppings. All but one are made in the same basic way. The exception is milk pizza dough, which is a quick baking powder–leavened dough.

Yeast doughs are easily enough made using the active dry yeast sold in every supermarket. You might seek out fast-acting yeast, available in specialty-food shops, which does not require proofing and, once dissolved, is mixed directly with the flour. It also reduces rising time by about 20 percent. As for flour, regular all-purpose (plain) flour is the only kind you need. But when you want a more robust dough, a little whole-wheat (wholemeal) flour, cornmeal or mashed potato will subtly alter the flavor and texture.

As the simple steps at right demonstrate, pizza dough takes more time than effort to make. Even when time is lacking, though, you can still make pizza. Prepare a double batch of dough in advance; tightly enclose balls of the dough in plastic wrap and freeze them; defrost at room temperature for several hours, or all day in the refrigerator. Or use one of the good-quality frozen pizza or bread doughs available at many supermarkets.

1. Dissolving the yeast.
In a small mixing bowl, stir together dry yeast and lukewarm water until the yeast granules dissolve. Leave at room temperature until yeast foams slightly and looks creamy, about 10 minutes.

2. Mixing dough in a processor.
If making dough with a food processor, fit with the metal blade and add the flour and any other dry ingredients to the work bowl. With the machine running, slowly pour the yeast mixture through the feed tube and continue processing just until the mixture forms a ball of dough that rides around on the blade. Proceed to step 4.

3. Mixing dough by hand.
If making the dough by hand, combine the flour and any other dry ingredients and heap in a mound on a work surface, or put in a large bowl. Make a well in the center, add the yeast mixture and stir with a fork in a circular motion, gradually incorporating the water until the dough forms.

4. Kneading the dough.
If the dough was mixed by hand, transfer it to a lightly floured work surface and knead lightly with the heel of your hand—pushing the dough forward and turning it slightly, then folding it back over and repeating—until smooth and elastic, about 10 minutes. If the dough was mixed in a processor, knead for only 1–2 minutes.

5. Letting the dough rise.
Lightly coat a large bowl with oil. Gather the dough into a ball, place it in the bowl and cover the bowl tightly with plastic wrap. Leave at room temperature to rise until doubled in bulk (above), 1–2 hours.

6. Punching down the dough.
Before shaping the pizza, transfer the risen dough to a lightly floured work surface and, using the heel of your hand, gently punch it down to deflate it slightly. Proceed with shaping, topping or filling, and baking the dough (see pages 14–15).

Basic Pizza Dough

Here is an all-purpose dough that complements both traditional and modern pizzas.

1 tablespoon active dry yeast
¾ cup plus 2 tablespoons (7 fl oz/210 ml) lukewarm
   water (105°F/40°C)
2¾ cups (11 oz/360 g) all-purpose (plain) flour, plus
   ½ cup (2 oz/60 g) for working
1 teaspoon salt
1 tablespoon extra-virgin olive oil

In a small bowl dissolve the yeast in the water and let stand until slightly foamy on top, about 10 minutes.

In a large bowl stir together the 2¾ cups (11 oz/ 360 g) flour and the salt and form into a mound. Make a well in the center and add the yeast mixture to the well. Using a fork and stirring in a circular motion, gradually pull the flour into the yeast mixture. Continue stirring until a dough forms.

Lightly flour a work surface with some of the ½ cup (2 oz/ 60 g) flour and transfer the dough to it. Using the heel of your hand, knead the dough until it is smooth and elastic, about 10 minutes. Form the dough into a ball.

Brush a large bowl with the oil and place the dough in it. Cover with plastic wrap and let rise at room temperature until doubled, 1–2 hours.

Turn the dough out onto a surface dusted with the remaining flour. Punch the dough down and, using your hand, begin to press it out gently into the desired shape. Then, place one hand in the center of the dough and, with the other hand, pull, lift and stretch the dough, gradually working your way all around the edge, until it is the desired thickness, about ¼ inch (6 mm) thick for a crusty pizza base and ½ inch (12 mm) thick for a softer one. Flip the dough over from time to time as you work with it. (Or roll out the dough with a rolling pin.) The dough should be slightly thinner in the middle than at the edge. Lift the edge of the pizza to form a slight rim.

Transfer the dough to a baker's peel or baking sheet, cover with a cotton towel and let rise again until almost doubled, about 20 minutes. Top and bake as directed in the individual recipes.

Makes 1¼ lb (600 g) dough, enough for a 12-inch (30-cm) thin-crust pizza or a 9-inch (24-cm) thick-crust pizza

Basic Pizza Dough

Herb Pizza Dough

Fresh or dried herbs add an accent of flavor and color to pizza dough. Good choices include oregano, basil, marjoram, chives, thyme, rosemary, sage, mint and fennel seeds, selected to highlight the ingredients that will top the pizza or fill the calzone. Do not go overboard on your selection: It is better to choose two or three complementary herbs, or even just one herb, rather than a large mixed bouquet of clashing flavors.

1 tablespoon active dry yeast
¾ cup plus 2 tablespoons (7 fl oz/210 ml) lukewarm water (105°F/40°C)
2¾ cups (11 oz/360 g) all-purpose (plain) flour, plus ½ cup (2 oz/60 g) for working
1 teaspoon salt
2 tablespoons minced mixed fresh herbs or 1 tablespoon mixed dried herbs
1 tablespoon extra-virgin olive oil

*P*roceed as directed for the basic pizza dough (recipe opposite), stirring the herbs together with the flour and salt.

Makes 1¼ lb (600 g) dough, enough for a 12-inch (30-cm) thin-crust pizza or a 9-inch (24-cm) thick-crust pizza

Herb Pizza Dough

Whole-Wheat Pizza Dough

Heavier and more flavorful than the standard dough, whole-wheat dough goes well with more robust pizza or calzone ingredients. Because of its increased fiber content, it will not, however, rise as high, producing a denser, chewier crust. If you want both flavor and lightness, use half whole-wheat flour and half all-purpose (plain) flour.

1 tablespoon active dry yeast
¾ cup plus 2 tablespoons (7 fl oz/210 ml) lukewarm water (105°F/40°C)
2¾ cups (11 oz/360 g) whole-wheat (wholemeal) flour, plus ½ cup (2 oz/60 g) for working
1 teaspoon salt
1 tablespoon extra-virgin olive oil

*P*roceed as directed for the basic pizza dough (recipe opposite), substituting whole-wheat flour for the all-purpose (plain) flour.

Makes 1¼ lb (600 g) dough, enough for a 12-inch (30-cm) thin-crust pizza or a 9-inch (24-cm) thick-crust pizza

Whole-Wheat Pizza Dough

11

Potato Pizza Dough

Mashed potato adds an earthy flavor to this dough, along with an appealingly crumbly texture—an effect you can increase, if you like, by using two potatoes and only 2 cups (8 oz/240 g) flour. The moisture content of potatoes varies, so keep a close eye on how much water you add to the dough: hold a little back if the dough seems too moist, or add a little more if it is too dry. Use this dough for four-cheese pizza (recipe on page 40) and onion ring pizza with potatoes (page 45), among others.

1 boiling potato, 5 oz (150 g)
1 tablespoon active dry yeast
¾ cup plus 2 tablespoons (7 fl oz/210 ml) lukewarm water (105°F/40°C)
2½ cups (10 oz/300 g) all-purpose (plain) flour, plus ½ cup (2 oz/60 g) for working
1 teaspoon salt
1 tablespoon extra-virgin olive oil

Boil the potato in water to cover until tender, 20–30 minutes; drain and peel while still hot.

Meanwhile, in a small bowl dissolve the yeast in the water and let stand until slightly foamy on top, about 10 minutes.

In a large bowl stir together the 2½ cups (10 oz/300 g) flour and the salt. Pass the hot peeled potato through a sieve into the bowl and form the mixture into a mound. Make a well in the center of the mound and add the yeast mixture to the well. Using a fork and stirring in a circular motion, gradually pull the flour and potato into the yeast mixture. Continue stirring until a dough forms.

Proceed as directed for the basic pizza dough (recipe on page 10).

Makes 1½ lb (700 g) dough, enough for a 12-inch (30-cm) thin-crust pizza or a 9-inch (24-cm) thick-crust pizza

Milk Pizza Dough

Potato Pizza Dough

Milk Pizza Dough

This soft, butter-enriched dough produces a thin, crisp crust that complements sweet toppings. The dough works particularly well for making smaller pizzas.

2¾ cups (11 oz/360 g) all-purpose (plain) flour, plus
   ½ cup (2 oz/60 g) for working
¾ cup (6 fl oz/180 ml) milk
5 tablespoons (2½ oz/75 g) unsalted butter, softened
1 teaspoon baking powder
1 teaspoon salt

*I*n a large bowl combine the 2¾ cups (11 oz/360 g) flour, milk, butter, baking powder and salt. Stir with a fork until a soft dough forms. Shape into a ball.
  Lightly flour a work surface with the remaining flour. Using a rolling pin, roll out the dough into a round ⅛ inch (3 mm) thick and about 12 inches (30 cm) in diameter. Flip it over occasionally as you roll it out. The dough should be slightly thinner in the middle than at the edge. When it is the correct size, lift the edge of the pizza to form a slight rim. Top and bake as directed in the individual recipes.

Makes 1¼ lb (600 g) dough, enough for a 12-inch (30-cm) pizza

Cornmeal Pizza Dough

To make this dough, select very fine-grind cornmeal, not the medium or coarse grind used for Italian polenta. As with the whole-wheat dough, the cornmeal will weigh down the flour, producing a heavier crust well-suited to hearty toppings, such as broccoli and garlic pizza (recipe on page 17) and prosciutto and egg pizza (page 66).

1 tablespoon active dry yeast
¾ cup plus 2 tablespoons (7 fl oz/210 ml) lukewarm
   water (105°F/40°C)
2½ cups (10 oz/300 g) all-purpose (plain) flour, plus
   ½ cup (2 oz/60 g) for working
⅓ cup (2 oz/60 g) fine yellow cornmeal
1 teaspoon salt
1 tablespoon extra-virgin olive oil

*I*n a small bowl dissolve the yeast in the water and let stand until slightly foamy on top, about 10 minutes.
  In a large bowl stir together the 2½ cups (10 oz/300 g) flour, the cornmeal and salt and form into a mound. Make a well in the center and add the yeast mixture to the well. Using a fork and stirring in a circular motion, gradually pull the flour into the yeast mixture. Continue stirring until a dough forms.
  Proceed as directed for the basic pizza dough (recipe on page 10).

Makes 1¼ lb (600 g) dough, enough for a 12-inch (30-cm) thin-crust pizza or a 9-inch (24-cm) thick-crust pizza

*Cornmeal
Pizza Dough*

SHAPING AND BAKING PIZZAS

Professional pointers that yield pizzeria-perfect results in the home kitchen

Every step of a pizza's final assembly and baking aims to produce the ideal combination of golden brown crust and bubbling-hot topping.

To this end, no single factor is more important than the oven's heat. Baking tiles or a baking stone, placed on the oven floor or on its lowest rack, best reproduce the intense, dry heat of a professional baker's oven. But to do this, the tiles or stone must be adequately preheated: Before you put the pizza into the oven, place an oven thermometer on the baking surface to check that its temperature matches the one called for in the recipe. If you don't have a baking stone or tiles, use a baking pan or sheet—or any other flat, heat-conductive surface.

Pizzas themselves are surprisingly simple to assemble. Dough is fairly pliant—enough so, indeed, to stand up well to the traditional Italian custom of shaping it into rounds by tossing and spinning it in the air. This practice, which limits the amount of direct pressure applied to the dough, is believed to yield the lightest crust. But you'll get fine results shaping the dough on a work surface, by hand or with a rolling pin, into whatever shapes you like.

Bear in mind, though, that the more elaborate your pizza's shape or toppings, the more awkward it might be to transfer it to or from the oven. Large pizzas may be shaped directly on a baker's peel that has been dusted with flour or cornmeal. Generously topped pizzas or large filled calzone (see sidebar, opposite) might do best on a pizza screen or baking sheet or in a baking pan.

1. Shaping the dough by hand.
Preheat an oven. If using a baking stone or tiles, place in the oven now. Having punched down a ball of pizza dough (see pages 8–9), use your hands to shape the ball of dough on a lightly floured work surface—gently pressing, lifting and stretching it to the desired flat shape and thickness. For a soft crust, press it out to a thickness of about ½ inch (12 mm); for a crisper crust, press it out to a thickness of about ¼ inch (6 mm). With your fingertips form a slightly raised rim.

2. Rolling out the dough.
Alternatively, use a rolling pin to flatten the dough, rolling it out into the desired shape. For a soft crust, roll it to a thickness of about ½ inch (12 mm); for a crisper crust, roll it to a thickness of about ¼ inch (6 mm). With your fingertips form a slightly raised rim.

14

3. Baking the pizza.
Transfer the dough to a floured tray, a rimless baking sheet or a flour- or cornmeal-dusted baker's peel. Leave at room temperature to rise again for about 20 minutes. Arrange the prepared topping ingredients on the pizza. Slide the pizza into the oven to bake.

4. Removing from the oven.
When the crust is golden brown and the topping is hot and bubbling, carefully push the baker's peel, baking sheet or large spatulas under the pizza and remove it from the oven. Transfer the pizza to a cutting board or metal serving pan.

5. Cutting the pizza.
If called for in a recipe, drizzle the hot pizza with a little olive oil for extra flavor and moistness. Pressing down firmly, roll a cutting wheel across the pizza (or use a knife) to cut it into individual slices. Serve immediately.

Use your imagination when making pizzas—there are no hard and fast rules. Try making them square, oval or any shape to fit a favorite platter. Feel free to shape small pizzas for individual servings, or tiny pizzas for hors d'oeuvres. Experiment with decorative edges, too. The pizza at left was made by simply pinching the rim with fingertips.

Making Calzone

The term *calzone*, Italian for "pantaloon," charmingly describes the shape of a pizza that has been transformed into a turnover. Virtually any recipe in this book can be made into a calzone. But the technique is best suited to containing those more abundant fillings that cannot neatly be served atop a pizza.

1. Rolling out the dough.
Prepare the dough as you would for a pizza. Form the risen dough into individual-serving balls. On a lightly floured surface, roll each ball of dough into a neat round about 6 inches (15 cm) in diameter. Alternatively, use your hands to shape the dough into a round.

2. Adding the filling.
Prepare the calzone filling as called for in the recipe. Mound the filling on top of the rolled-out dough, covering roughly half of the dough's surface and leaving a generous rim.

3. Sealing the calzone.
Using a brush dipped in water, lightly moisten the edges of the dough. Fold the uncovered portion over the filling, gently stretching it to cover the ingredients completely, forming a semicircle. Firmly press and crimp the edges together to seal securely.

Broccoli and Garlic Pizza
PIZZA AI BROCCOLI

cornmeal pizza dough (*recipe on page 13*)
1¼ lb (600 g) broccoli
4 tablespoons (2 fl oz/60 ml) extra-virgin olive oil
3 cloves garlic, chopped
10 oz (300 g) fresh plum (Roma) tomatoes, peeled and chopped, or canned plum tomatoes with their liquid, chopped
salt and freshly ground pepper
1 tablespoon raisins

A scattering of raisins adds a refreshing sweet-tart taste to this garlicky specialty from southern Italy.

Make the pizza dough. Preheat an oven to 450°F (220°C). If using a baking stone or tiles, place in the oven now.

Separate the broccoli florets from the stems. Cut the florets and the tender stems into ¾-inch (2-cm) pieces; discard the large tough stems. Add the tender stems to boiling salted water and cook for 3 minutes. Add the florets and cook for 1 minute. The broccoli should still be crisp. Drain and immediately immerse in ice water. Drain again and separate the stems and florets; set aside.

Warm 3 tablespoons of the oil in a saucepan over medium heat. Add the garlic and sauté until translucent, about 1 minute. Add the tomatoes, reduce heat to low, cover partially and cook until most of the liquid evaporates, about 10 minutes. Add the stems and cook until tender, about 10 minutes. Season with salt and pepper.

Shape the pizza dough and cover with the tomato sauce. Transfer to the oven and bake for 10 minutes. Remove from the oven and sprinkle with the broccoli florets and raisins. Quickly return to the oven, reduce the temperature to 400°F (200°C) and bake until the crust is golden, about 10 minutes. Drizzle the remaining 1 tablespoon oil over the top and serve immediately.

Serves 4

Onion and Goat Cheese Pizza
PIZZA DI CIPOLLE E CAPRINO

potato pizza dough (recipe on
  page 12)
4 large onions, thinly sliced
1 tablespoon unsalted butter
3 tablespoons extra-virgin olive oil
1 tablespoon sugar
3 tablespoons red wine vinegar
salt
6 oz (180 g) fresh goat cheese,
  crumbled
½ cup (2 oz/60 g) chopped walnuts

The onions that top this pizza are cooked with sugar and vinegar until they are almost caramelized, resulting in a sweet-tart flavor perfectly suited to the fresh, creamy goat cheese that covers the dough. Shape four individual pizzas and serve them as main courses for a light lunch.

Make the pizza dough. Preheat an oven to 450°F (220°C). If using a baking stone or tiles, place in the oven now.

  In a frying pan over low heat, combine the onions, butter and 2 tablespoons of the oil. Cover and cook, stirring often, until the onions are very soft, about 30 minutes, adding a little water occasionally if needed to prevent sticking. Add the sugar and vinegar and continue to cook until the vinegar evaporates, about 3 minutes. Add salt to taste.

  Shape the pizza dough into one large round or 4 individual rounds. Cover with the cheese. Scatter the walnuts over the top and then the onions. Transfer to the oven and bake for 10 minutes. Reduce the oven temperature to 400°F (200°C) and bake until the crust is golden, about 10 minutes. Drizzle the remaining 1 tablespoon oil over the top and serve immediately.

Serves 4

Marinated Zucchini Pizza
PIZZA ALLE ZUCCHINE

herb pizza dough (recipe on page 11)

5 cups (40 fl oz/1.2 l) olive oil or vegetable oil for deep-frying

4 zucchini (courgettes), about 13 oz (420 g) total weight, cut into slices ⅛ inch (3 mm) thick

¼ cup (2 fl oz/60 ml) red wine vinegar

3 cloves garlic, chopped

salt and freshly ground pepper

1 handful of fresh basil leaves, torn into strips

Cooking thin zucchini slices first in olive oil and then in vinegar creates the delicious illusion that they have marinated in those ingredients. The "marinating" technique also works well with eggplants (aubergines). Covering the pizza with half green zucchini and half yellow zucchini, alternating the slices, makes a tantalizing presentation.

Make the pizza dough. Preheat an oven to 450°F (220°C). If using a baking stone or tiles, place in the oven now.

Pour the oil into a deep frying pan and heat to 350°F (170°C). Slip the zucchini slices into the oil, a few at a time, and fry until barely golden, about 2 minutes. Transfer with a slotted spoon to paper towels to drain. When all of the slices have been fried, pour off all but about 1 tablespoon of the oil. Return the fried zucchini to the pan and pour in the vinegar. Place over medium heat, add the garlic and cook until the vinegar evaporates and the zucchini begins to darken, about 5 minutes. Season to taste with salt and pepper.

Shape the pizza dough and cover with the zucchini. Transfer to the oven and bake for 10 minutes. Reduce the oven temperature to 400°F (200°C) and bake until the crust is golden, about 10 minutes. Scatter the basil over the top and serve immediately.

Serves 4

Black Olive Pizza
Pizza alle Olive

herb pizza dough (recipe on page 11)
4 tablespoons (2 fl oz/60 ml) extra-
   virgin olive oil
4 cloves garlic
1¼ lb (600 g) fresh plum (Roma)
   tomatoes, peeled and chopped, or
   canned plum tomatoes with their
   liquid, chopped
2 tablespoons fresh thyme leaves
salt and freshly ground pepper
7 oz (210 g) mozzarella cheese, thinly
   sliced
20 Gaeta or Greek black olives, pitted

An herb-flavored pizza dough distinguishes this modern-day version of a Roman classic, which conceals its cheese beneath the tomato sauce. For a more authentic pie, use basic pizza dough (recipe on page 10). Shape the dough into four individual squares, if you like, for a rustic look.

Make the pizza dough. Preheat an oven to 450°F (220°C). If using a baking stone or tiles, place in the oven now.

Warm 3 tablespoons of the oil in a frying pan over low heat. Add the garlic and sauté, stirring occasionally, until translucent, about 2 minutes. Add the tomatoes, cover partially and cook, stirring occasionally, until the liquid evaporates, about 40 minutes. Add the thyme and season to taste with salt and pepper.

Shape the pizza dough into one large pizza or 4 individual pizzas. Cover with the mozzarella. Evenly distribute the tomato mixture on top and then decorate with the olives. Transfer to the oven and bake for 10 minutes. Reduce the oven temperature to 400°F (200°C) and bake until the crust is golden, about 10 minutes. Drizzle with the remaining 1 tablespoon oil and serve immediately.

Serves 4

Goat Cheese, Olive and Pesto Pizza
PIZZA AL PESTO

basic pizza dough (recipe on page 10)
¾ cup (1 oz/30 g) fresh basil leaves
salt
8 tablespoons (4 fl oz/120 ml) extra-
   virgin olive oil
½ cup (2 oz/60 g) freshly grated
   Parmesan cheese
¼ cup (1 oz/30 g) freshly grated
   Romano cheese
3 tablespoons (1 oz/30 g) pine nuts
6 oz (180 g) fresh goat cheese, sliced
2 oz (60 g) Gaeta or Greek black
   olives, pitted and sliced
freshly ground pepper

The topping is inspired by the Ligurian cuisine of north-western Italy. But lovers of Greek food are also likely to find the aromatic, pungent combination of ingredients happily familiar. If you like, add a garlic clove when puréeing the basil mixture. For a less sharp-tasting sauce, use Swiss cheese instead of the Parmesan and Romano.

Make the pizza dough. Preheat an oven to 450°F (220°C). If using a baking stone or tiles, place in the oven now.

In a blender or in a food processor fitted with the metal blade, place the basil leaves and a little salt. (The salt keeps the basil from darkening.) Process until finely chopped. With the motor running, add 6 tablespoons (3 fl oz/90 ml) of the oil, the Parmesan, Romano and pine nuts, and continue to process until a smooth, creamy mixture forms.

Shape the pizza dough and cover with the goat cheese. Drizzle the remaining 2 tablespoons oil over the cheese and then pour half of the basil mixture evenly onto the pizza. Scatter the olives over the top and season to taste with pepper. Transfer the pizza to the oven and bake for 10 minutes. Reduce the oven temperature to 400°F (200°C) and bake until the crust is golden, about 10 minutes. Pour the remaining basil mixture evenly over the top and serve immediately.

Serves 4

Fontina Cheese Pizza

PIZZA DI FONTINA

cornmeal pizza dough (recipe on
   page 13)
10 oz (300 g) Fontina cheese, thinly
   sliced
¾ cup (6 fl oz/180 ml) dry white wine
½ cup (2 oz/60 g) freshly grated
   Parmesan cheese
3 egg yolks, lightly beaten
salt and freshly ground pepper

*The topping—a rich and creamy blend of Fontina, Parmesan
and egg yolks—is especially good on miniature rounds of
pizza dough, baked up fresh as an hors d'oeuvre to serve with
white wine or cocktails. You can also scatter some crumbled,
crisply cooked bacon or cooked sausage over the pizza dough
before adding the cheese.*

Make the pizza dough. Preheat an oven to 450°F
(220°C). If using a baking stone or tiles, place in the
oven now.

Combine the Fontina and wine in a heatproof bowl
and place in a saucepan filled partway with almost
boiling water, to create a bain-marie. Once the cheese
melts, add the Parmesan cheese and egg yolks and stir
until the mixture is creamy and thickens, about 5
minutes. Do not let the mixture boil. Remove from the
heat and season to taste with salt and pepper.

Shape the pizza dough into one large round or small
hors d'oeuvre–sized rounds. Spoon the Fontina mixture
evenly over the top. Transfer to the oven and bake for 10
minutes. Reduce the oven temperature to 400°F (200°C)
and bake until the crust is golden, about 10 minutes.
Serve immediately.

Serves 4, or more as hors d'oeuvres

Eggplant and Smoked Trout Pizza
PIZZA ALLE MELANZANE

herb pizza dough (*recipe on page 11*)
1 yellow bell pepper (capsicum)
2 eggplants (aubergines), about 10 oz
   (300 g) total weight, thinly sliced
   lengthwise
4 tablespoons (2 fl oz/60 ml) extra-
   virgin olive oil
1 smoked trout fillet
1 teaspoon freshly grated horseradish
salt

In this up-to-date recipe, the gentle, smoky taste of the trout complements the eggplant's earthy flavor, and both are highlighted by a hint of hot-sweet grated horseradish. You can substitute milder, sweeter zucchini (courgettes) for the eggplants, in which case leave out the horseradish.

Make the pizza dough. Preheat a broiler (griller). Preheat an oven to 450°F (220°C). If using a baking stone or tiles, place in the oven now.

Cut the bell pepper in half and remove the stem, seeds and ribs. Slice into long strips about ½ inch (12 mm) wide. Brush the pepper strips and eggplant slices on both sides with 2 tablespoons of the oil and arrange them in a flameproof pan. Slip under the broiler and broil (grill), turning once, until tender when pierced, about 2 minutes on each side. Remove from the broiler and set aside.

Place the trout fillet in a bowl and mash with a fork. Stir in the remaining 2 tablespoons oil and the horseradish.

Shape the pizza dough and cover with the mashed trout, eggplant and bell pepper. Season to taste with salt. Transfer to the oven and bake for 10 minutes. Reduce the temperature to 400°F (200°C) and bake until the crust is golden, about 10 minutes. Serve immediately.

Serves 4

Pizza Margherita

basic pizza dough (recipe on page 10)

7 oz (210 g) mozzarella cheese, thinly
  sliced

8 fresh plum (Roma) tomatoes, peeled
  and chopped, or canned plum
  tomatoes, drained and chopped

1 handful of fresh basil leaves

salt and freshly ground pepper

4 tablespoons (2 fl oz/60 ml) extra-
  virgin olive oil

Now a well-loved and widely traveled variety of pizza, this combination was the inspiration of 19th-century Neapolitan pizza maker Raffaele Esposito, who created it to honor Queen Margherita, wife of Italy's King Umberto I, on a royal visit to Naples in 1889.

Make the pizza dough. Preheat an oven to 450°F (220°C). If using a baking stone or tiles, place in the oven now.

  Shape the pizza dough into one large round or 4 individual rounds. Cover with the mozzarella and then the tomatoes. Scatter the basil over the top. Season to taste with salt and pepper and drizzle 3 tablespoons of the oil over the top. Transfer to the oven and bake for 10 minutes. Reduce the oven temperature to 400°F (200°C) and bake until the crust is golden, about 10 minutes. Drizzle the remaining 1 tablespoon oil over the top and serve immediately.

Serves 4

Potato, Onion and Rosemary Pizza

PIZZA DI PATATE

whole-wheat pizza dough (*recipe on page 11*)
2 boiling potatoes
1 onion, sliced paper-thin
2 tablespoons fresh rosemary, chopped if desired
4 tablespoons (2 fl oz/60 ml) extra-virgin olive oil
salt and freshly ground pepper

A robust specialty of the pizzeria La Baia in Milan, this recipe may also be made with basic pizza dough (recipe on page 10). Crumbled crisp bacon scattered over the onions would be a delicious addition.

Make the pizza dough. Preheat an oven to 450°F (220°C). If using a baking stone or tiles, place in the oven now.

Boil the potatoes in salted water until tender, about 30 minutes. Drain, peel and let cool, then slice thinly.

Shape the pizza dough and cover with the potatoes. Arrange the onions on top and sprinkle with the rosemary. Drizzle 3 tablespoons of the oil over the top. Season to taste with salt and pepper.

Transfer to the oven and bake for 10 minutes. Reduce the temperature to 400°F (200°C) and bake until the crust is golden, about 10 minutes. Drizzle the remaining 1 tablespoon oil over the top and serve immediately.

Serves 4

Radicchio, Bacon and Onion Pizza
PIZZA AL RADICCHIO

basic pizza dough (*recipe on page 10*)
4 heads radicchio, cut in half
  lengthwise
3 tablespoons extra-virgin olive oil
2 onions, thinly sliced
4 slices bacon
salt and freshly ground pepper

You can replace the radicchio with Belgian endive (chicory/witloof), broiled in the same way.

Make the pizza dough. Preheat a broiler (griller). Preheat an oven to 450°F (220°C). If using a baking stone or tiles, place in the oven now.

Brush both sides of the radicchio halves with 1½ tablespoons of the oil and place in a flameproof pan. Slip under the broiler and broil (grill) for 2 minutes. Turn and broil the second side for 2 minutes. Remove and discard the charred outer leaves as they are bitter; set the radicchio aside. Brush the onion slices on both sides with the remaining 1½ tablespoons oil, arrange in the same pan and broil for 1 minute on each side, turning once. Remove and set aside. Then arrange the bacon slices in the pan and broil until lightly golden and crisp, about 2 minutes on each side.

Shape the pizza dough into one large pizza or 4 individual pizzas. Cover with the radicchio. Arrange the bacon slices on top and then cover with the onions. Season to taste with salt and pepper. Transfer to the oven and bake for 10 minutes. Reduce the oven temperature to 400°F (200°C) and bake until the crust is golden, about 10 minutes.

Serves 4

Roasted Bell Pepper Pizza

PIZZA AI PEPERONI

herb pizza dough *(recipe on page 11)*

3 yellow and/or red bell peppers
(capsicums)

4 tablespoons (2 fl oz/60 ml) extra-
virgin olive oil

½ cup (2 oz/60 g) fine dried
bread crumbs

3 cloves garlic, minced

3 large tomatoes, peeled and thinly
sliced

2 tablespoons well-drained capers

salt and freshly ground pepper

This preparation also works well with eggplant (aubergine),
punctured in several places with a fork and roasted until soft,
following the instructions given below for the peppers.

Make the pizza dough. Preheat an oven to 450°F
(220°C). If using a baking stone or tiles, place in the
oven now.

Arrange the bell peppers on a baking pan and bake
until the skins are blackened a little, about 20 minutes.
Remove from the oven, cover with a cotton towel and let
stand until cool enough to handle. Using your fingertips,
rub them gently until the skins loosen, then peel them.
Remove the stems, seeds and ribs and cut the peppers
into long strips about ⅜ inch (1 cm) wide. Set aside.
Leave the oven set at 450°F (220°C).

Warm 3 tablespoons of the oil in a frying pan over medium
heat. Add the bread crumbs and garlic and fry, stirring
continuously, until golden, about 3 minutes. Set aside.

Shape the pizza dough and cover with the pepper
strips. Arrange the tomato slices on top and sprinkle
with the capers. Season to taste with salt and pepper.
Transfer the pizza to the oven and bake for 10 minutes.
Reduce the oven temperature to 400°F (200°C) and bake
until the crust is golden, about 10 minutes. Drizzle with
the remaining 1 tablespoon oil and sprinkle with the
fried bread crumbs. Serve immediately.

Serves 4

Gorgonzola and Walnut Pizza
PIZZA AL GORGONZOLA

whole-wheat pizza dough *(recipe on page 11)*

4 tablespoons (2 fl oz/60 ml) extra-virgin olive oil

10 oz (300 g) Gorgonzola cheese, sliced

⅔ cup (2 oz/60 g) walnut halves

1 tablespoon lemon zest

freshly ground pepper

Although the pizza itself is contemporary, the pairing of blue-veined cheese with walnuts is a time-honored classic. Offer it after dinner, with a glass of Vin Santo or port. Substitute another blue-veined cheese of your choice, such as Roquefort or Stilton, or a creamy Camembert or Brie pared of the white rind. Pecans or almonds can stand in for the walnuts.

Make the pizza dough. Preheat an oven to 450°F (220°C). If using a baking stone or tiles, place in the oven now.

Shape the pizza dough and drizzle 2 tablespoons of the oil over the top. Cover with the Gorgonzola and then with the walnuts. Sprinkle evenly with the lemon zest and drizzle 1 tablespoon oil over the top. Season to taste with pepper. Transfer the pizza to the oven and bake for 10 minutes. Reduce the oven temperature to 400°F (200°C) and bake until the crust is golden, about 10 minutes. Drizzle the remaining 1 tablespoon oil over the top and serve immediately.

Serves 4

Four-Cheese Pizza
PIZZA AI QUATTRO FORMAGGI

potato pizza dough (recipe on
  page 12)
2 oz (60 g) Gorgonzola cheese
2 oz (60 g) fresh goat cheese
2 oz (60 g) Fontina cheese
2 oz (60 g) mozzarella cheese
1 tablespoon extra-virgin olive oil

*Like four different pizzas in one, this recipe presents a
quartet of distinctive toppings. Feel free to substitute whatever
cheeses are available and appealing to you. If you like, roll a
few scraps of pizza dough into long, thin strips and place
them on top of the crust to divide one cheese from the next.
You can also scatter each cheese over the pizza's entire
surface, letting them melt together.*

Make the pizza dough. Preheat an oven to 450°F
(220°C). If using a baking stone or tiles, place in the
oven now. Place the Gorgonzola and goat cheeses in the
freezer for 30 minutes, to make them easier to slice.

  Thinly slice the Gorgonzola, goat, Fontina and
mozzarella cheeses. Shape the pizza dough and top with
the cheeses. Transfer to the oven and bake for 10
minutes. Reduce the oven temperature to 400°F (200°C)
and bake until the crust is golden, about 10 minutes.
Drizzle the oil over the top and serve immediately.

Serves 4

Asparagus and Ham Pizza

PIZZA AGLI ASPARAGI

whole-wheat pizza dough (recipe on
  page 11)
10 oz (300 g) trimmed asparagus tips
6 oz (180 g) cooked ham, thinly sliced
6 oz (180 g) mozzarella cheese, sliced
4 tablespoons (2 fl oz/60 ml) extra-
  virgin olive oil
freshly ground pepper
6 tablespoons (1½ oz/45 g) freshly
  grated Parmesan cheese

*This recipe presents a classic combination of ingredients
most commonly seen in a favorite gratin dish. You can, if
you wish, use Gruyère or Emmenthaler cheese in place of
the mozzarella, and prosciutto for the ham. Swiss chard
(silverbeet) and spinach are other good vegetable choices.*

Make the pizza dough. Preheat an oven to 450°F
(220°C). If using a baking stone or tiles, place in the
oven now.

   Have a bowl of ice water ready. Bring a saucepan
filled with salted water to a boil. Add the asparagus tips
and blanch for 3 minutes. Drain, immediately immerse
in the ice water and drain again.

   Shape the pizza dough. Arrange the asparagus, ham
and mozzarella on top. Drizzle 3 tablespoons of the oil
over the top and season to taste with pepper. Transfer
the pizza to the oven and bake for 10 minutes. Remove
from the oven, sprinkle with the Parmesan and quickly
return to the oven. Reduce the temperature to 400°F
(200°C) and bake until the crust is golden, about 10
minutes. Drizzle the remaining 1 tablespoon oil over the
top and serve immediately.

Serves 4

Onion Ring Pizza with Golden Potatoes
PIZZA ALLE CIPOLLE FRITTE

potato pizza dough *(recipe on page 12)*

2 tablespoons all-purpose (plain) flour

1 onion, sliced and separated into rings

5 cups (40 fl oz/1.2 l) olive oil or vegetable oil for deep-frying

½ cup (4 fl oz/120 ml) extra-virgin olive oil

4 boiling potatoes, peeled and cut into ¾-inch (2-cm) dice

3 cloves garlic

1 handful of fresh sage leaves

salt and freshly ground pepper

1 tablespoon sesame seeds

Save some sage leaves to use as garnish, if you like.

Make the pizza dough. Preheat an oven to 450°F (220°C). If using a baking stone or tiles, place in the oven now.

Place the flour in a paper bag and add the onion rings. Shake the bag well to coat the onion rings fully, then take them out one by one, shaking off any excess flour.

Heat the 5 cups (40 fl oz/1.2 l) oil in a deep frying pan to about 350°F (170°C). Fry the onion rings, a few at a time, until they turn a deep gold, about 5 minutes. Transfer to paper towels to drain.

In a large frying pan heat the ½ cup (4 fl oz/120 ml) extra-virgin olive oil over medium heat. Add the potatoes, garlic and sage and cook, stirring occasionally, until the potatoes are a deep golden color, about 20 minutes. Transfer to paper towels to drain. Discard the garlic and sage; season the potatoes with salt and pepper.

Shape the pizza dough and cover with the potatoes, onion rings and sesame seeds. Transfer the pizza to the oven and bake for 10 minutes. Reduce the oven temperature to 400°F (200°C) and bake until the crust is golden, about 10 minutes. Serve immediately.

Serves 4

Spinach and Goat Cheese Pizza
PIZZA DI SPINACI

cornmeal pizza dough (recipe on
  page 13)
1¼ lb (600 g) spinach, trimmed and
  washed
4 tablespoons (2 fl oz/60 ml) extra-
  virgin olive oil
salt and freshly ground pepper
2 eggs, lightly beaten
½ teaspoon freshly grated nutmeg
6 oz (180 g) fresh goat cheese

*The cheese is blended with the vegetables and eggs in this
pizza, creating an almost soufflélike topping. Swiss chard
(silverbeet) leaves, without the ribs, can be used in place of
the spinach, and you can substitute ricotta if you'd prefer
a less tangy cheese.*

Make the pizza dough. Preheat an oven to 450°F
(220°C). If using a baking stone or tiles, place in the
oven now.

Have a bowl of ice water ready. Bring a saucepan filled
with salted water to a boil, add the spinach and blanch
for 2 minutes. Drain, immediately immerse in the ice
water and drain again. Squeeze the spinach dry.

In a frying pan over medium heat, warm 2 tablespoons
of the oil. Add the spinach and sauté, stirring often, for
about 3 minutes. Season to taste with salt and pepper.
Remove from the heat and cool slightly, then stir in the
eggs, nutmeg and cheese.

Shape the pizza dough and drizzle with 1 tablespoon
of the oil. Cover with the spinach mixture. Transfer the
pizza to the oven and bake for 10 minutes. Reduce the
oven temperature to 400°F (200°C) and bake until the
crust is golden, about 10 minutes. Drizzle with the
remaining 1 tablespoon oil and serve immediately.

Serves 4

Curried Vegetable Pizza
PIZZA AL CURRY DI VERDURE

basic pizza dough (recipe on page 10)
⅓ cup (2 oz/60 g) raisins
4 tablespoons (2 fl oz/60 ml) extra-virgin olive oil
1 onion, thinly sliced
1 eggplant (aubergine), about 6 oz (180 g), cut into ½-inch (12-mm) dice
2 green chili peppers such as jalapeños or poblanos, seeded and chopped
3 fresh plum (Roma) tomatoes, peeled and chopped, or canned plum tomatoes with their liquid, chopped
1 potato, peeled and cut into ½-inch (12-mm) dice
1 Golden Delicious apple, peeled, cored and diced
1 tablespoon curry powder
salt and freshly ground pepper
6 tablespoons (2 oz/60 g) pine nuts

Italy meets India in a spicy topping mellowed by the sweetness of apple and raisins. Double the curry powder if you want a more fiery topping, and experiment with the vegetable combination by using zucchini (courgettes), broccoli, cauliflower and bell peppers (capsicums).

Make the pizza dough. In a small bowl, soak the raisins in water to cover for 30 minutes. Meanwhile, preheat an oven to 450°F (220°C). If using a baking stone or tiles, place in the oven now.

In a frying pan over medium heat, warm the oil. Add the onion and fry until lightly golden, about 5 minutes. Add the eggplant, chilies, tomatoes, potato, apple and curry powder and stir well. Cover partially and cook over low heat until very tender, about 30 minutes. If the mixture begins to stick to the pan bottom, add a few tablespoons water. Season to taste with salt and pepper.

Drain the raisins and add them to the frying pan along with the pine nuts. Cook, stirring occasionally, for another 2 minutes.

Shape the pizza dough and cover with the curried vegetables. Transfer the pizza to the oven and bake for 10 minutes. Reduce the oven temperature to 400°F (200°C) and bake until the crust is golden, about 10 minutes. Serve immediately.

Serves 4

Neapolitan Pizza
Pizza alla Napoletana

basic pizza dough (recipe on page 10)

7 oz (210 g) mozzarella cheese, thinly sliced

4 flat anchovy fillets in oil, drained and cut in half lengthwise

8 fresh plum (Roma) tomatoes, peeled and chopped, or canned plum tomatoes, drained and chopped

1 tablespoon dried oregano

salt and freshly ground pepper

4 tablespoons (2 fl oz/60 ml) extra-virgin olive oil

Along with Margherita pizza (recipe on page 30), this specialty of Naples is one of the most popular in Italy—a robust-tasting yet well-balanced combination of pizza dough, fresh tomatoes and anchovies. For a twist on the classic, bake miniature pizzas and serve them as an hors d'oeuvre. If you're not partial to the fish, substitute capers or olives, which transforms the recipe into a Roman-style pizza.

Make the pizza dough. Preheat an oven to 450°F (220°C). If using a baking stone or tiles, place in the oven now.

Shape the pizza dough into one large round or small hors d'oeuvre–sized rounds. Cover with the mozzarella. Top with the anchovies and then cover with the tomatoes. Sprinkle the oregano and salt and pepper to taste over the top. Drizzle 3 tablespoons of the oil evenly over the top. Transfer to the oven and bake for 10 minutes. Reduce the oven temperature to 400°F (200°C) and bake until the crust is golden, about 10 minutes. Drizzle the remaining 1 tablespoon oil over the top and serve immediately.

Serves 4, or more as hors d'oeuvres

Fresh Herb Pizza

Pizza alle Erbe

potato pizza dough (*recipe on page 12*)

4 tablespoons (2 fl oz/60 ml) extra-virgin olive oil

1 tablespoon minced fresh rosemary

1 tablespoon minced fresh marjoram

1 tablespoon minced fresh chives

1 tablespoon minced fresh basil

1 tablespoon chopped onion

1 teaspoon minced garlic

salt and freshly ground pepper

With so many different fresh herbs commonly available in supermarkets today, it's easy to shop for this contemporary recipe, which enhances the herbs' flavors with olive oil and garlic. Serve the pizza as an appetizer, on its own as a simple main course, or accompany it with sun-ripened tomatoes or other salads. Feel free to use your own favorite fresh herbs. Or substitute dried herbs, halving the quantities, or mixed whole dried spice seeds such as fennel, coriander or cumin, using only 1 tablespoon seeds in all.

Make the pizza dough. Preheat an oven to 450°F (220°C). If using a baking stone or tiles, place in the oven now.

On a lightly floured board, knead 2 tablespoons of the oil and the rosemary into the already-made pizza dough for 1 or 2 minutes.

Shape the pizza dough and sprinkle evenly with all the remaining herbs and the onion and garlic. Drizzle the remaining 2 tablespoons oil over the top. Season to taste with salt and pepper. Transfer the pizza to the oven and bake for 10 minutes. Reduce the oven temperature to 400°F (200°C) and bake until the crust is golden, about 10 minutes. Serve immediately.

Serves 4

Pizza Marinara

basic pizza dough (recipe on page 10)
8 cloves garlic, minced
1 teaspoon dried oregano
salt and freshly ground pepper
4 tablespoons (2 fl oz/60 ml) extra-
  virgin olive oil

Italian mariners assembled these simple pizzas during long ocean voyages, using the only ingredients that stored well aboard ship: olive oil, garlic and dried oregano. Bake as one large pizza or individual bite-sized portions, to serve as an hors d'oeuvre or as a companion to soups and salads.

Make the pizza dough. Preheat an oven to 450°F (220°C). If using a baking stone or tiles, place in the oven now.

Shape the pizza dough into one large round or small hors d'oeuvre–sized rounds. Sprinkle with the garlic, oregano and salt and pepper to taste. Drizzle 3 tablespoons of the oil evenly over the top. Transfer to the oven and bake for 10 minutes. Reduce the oven temperature to 400°F (200°C) and bake until the crust is golden, about 10 minutes. Drizzle the remaining 1 tablespoon oil over the top and serve immediately.

Serves 4, or more as hors d'oeuvres

Shrimp Pizza with Sweet Paprika

PIZZA AI GAMBERI

herb pizza dough *(recipe on page 11)*

¼ lb (120 g) Swiss cheese, thinly sliced

½ cup (4 fl oz/120 ml) milk

10 oz (300 g) shrimp, peeled and deveined

4 tablespoons (2 fl oz/60 ml) extra-virgin olive oil

1 teaspoon paprika

2 tablespoons chopped fresh chives

An elegant first course for dinner, or excellent on its own as a light meal, this pizza is international in its inspiration— combining fresh shrimp with Swiss cheese and a hint of sweet Hungarian or Spanish paprika.

Make the pizza dough. While the dough is rising, arrange the cheese slices in a shallow bowl. Pour the milk over them and let stand for about 2 hours, turning the slices over occasionally.

Preheat an oven to 450°F (220°C). If using a baking stone or tiles, place in the oven now.

Shape the pizza dough into one large round or 4 individual rounds. Scatter the shrimp over the top. Drizzle 3 tablespoons of the oil over the shrimp. Transfer to the oven and bake for 10 minutes. Meanwhile, drain off the milk from the cheese. Remove the pizza from the oven. Lay the cheese over the shrimp and sprinkle with the paprika. Quickly return the pizza to the oven, reduce the temperature to 400°F (200°C) and bake until the crust is golden, about 10 minutes. Drizzle the remaining 1 tablespoon oil over the top, sprinkle with the chives and serve immediately.

Serves 4

Tuna and Egg Pizza

PIZZA AL TONNO

potato pizza dough (*recipe on
  page 12*)

2 large tomatoes, peeled and chopped

10 oz (300 g) canned tuna in olive oil,
  drained and flaked

2 tablespoons well-drained capers

4 tablespoons (2 fl oz/60 ml) extra-
  virgin olive oil

salt and freshly ground pepper

2 eggs, hard-cooked and sliced

1 tablespoon flat-leaf (Italian) parsley,
  minced

*A favorite Roman recipe, this pizza nonetheless recalls the
classic combination of ingredients found in a French niçoise
salad, particularly when made with a potato pizza dough.
Canned salmon makes an excellent substitute for the tuna.*

Make the pizza dough. Preheat an oven to 450°F
(220°C). If using a baking stone or tiles, place in the
oven now.

  Shape the pizza dough and cover with the tomatoes.
Evenly distribute the tuna and capers over the tomatoes.
Drizzle 3 tablespoons of the oil over the top. Transfer to
the oven and bake for 10 minutes. Remove from the
oven. Season to taste with salt and pepper, arrange the
egg slices on top and sprinkle with the parsley. Quickly
return the pizza to the oven, reduce the temperature to
400°F (200°C) and bake until the crust is golden, about
10 minutes. Drizzle with the remaining 1 tablespoon oil
and serve immediately.

Serves 4

Smoked Salmon and Fennel Pizza

PIZZA AL SALMONE AFFUMICATO

basic pizza dough (recipe on page 10)
10 oz (300 g) smoked salmon, thinly
  sliced
1 fennel bulb, sliced paper-thin
4 tablespoons (2 fl oz/60 ml) extra-
  virgin olive oil
salt

Smoked salmon became a fashionable topping thanks to the trendsetting new American approach to pizza, particularly at places like chef Wolfgang Puck's Spago restaurant in Los Angeles. The mild, sweet anisey flavor of fresh fennel goes nicely with the salmon, as does thinly sliced onion. For extra elegance, top the pizza with a scattering of caviar.

Make the pizza dough. Preheat an oven to 450°F (220°C). If using a baking stone or tiles, place in the oven now.

  Shape the pizza dough. Transfer to the oven and bake for 10 minutes. Remove from the oven. Cover with the smoked salmon slices. Top with the fennel slices. Drizzle 3 tablespoons of the oil over the top and sprinkle with a little salt. Quickly return the pizza to the oven, reduce the temperature to 400°F (200°C) and bake until the crust is golden, about 10 minutes. Drizzle with the remaining 1 tablespoon oil and serve immediately.

Serves 4

Fried Pizzas with Prosciutto
Pizze Fritte

basic pizza dough (*recipe on page 10*)
5 cups (40 fl oz/1.2 l) olive oil or
   vegetable oil for deep-frying
7 oz (210 g) prosciutto, thinly sliced

Small, deep-fried disks of pizza dough are a favorite snack or hors d'oeuvre in the Emilia-Romagna region of northern Italy, where they are often topped after cooking with thin slices of prosciutto, the world-famous ham from nearby Parma. If you prefer, bake the disks instead of frying them: Preheat an oven to 450°F (220°C) and bake for 10 minutes, then reduce the heat to 400°F (200°C) and bake until golden, about 10 minutes.

Make the pizza dough and divide it into 8 equal pieces.

Preheat an oven to 250°F (120°C). On a floured work surface, use the palms of your hands to shape each piece into a log about 1 inch (2.5 cm) thick. Cut each log crosswise into 1½-inch (4-cm) pieces. On the floured surface roll out each piece of dough into a disk about ⅛ inch (3 mm) thick and 4 inches (10 cm) in diameter.

Pour the oil into a deep frying pan and heat to 350°F (170°C). Slip the disks into the hot oil, a few at a time, and fry until they puff and turn pale gold, about 3 minutes. Transfer them with a slotted spoon to paper towels to drain, then place in the oven with the door slightly ajar to keep warm until serving. Repeat with the remaining disks. Top each pizza with a slice of prosciutto and serve immediately.

Makes about 30 pizzas

Sausage and Apple Pizza
PIZZA ALLE SALSICCE E MELE

whole-wheat pizza dough (recipe on
page 11)

2 tablespoons extra-virgin olive oil

10 oz (300 g) sweet Italian sausages,
cut into slices ⅜ inch (1 cm) thick

2 tablespoons unsalted butter

4 Golden Delicious apples, peeled,
cored and cut into 1-inch (2.5-cm)
pieces

2 tablespoons coarse-grain French
mustard

*This pizza is from the Italian Alto Adige region, but its
savory-sweet toppings point northward toward Austria.
Smoked ham, in place of the sausage, would be just as good.
Use any high-quality, French-style coarse-grain mustard,
such as moutarde de Meaux.*

Make the pizza dough. Preheat an oven to 450°F
(220°C). If using a baking stone or tiles, place in the
oven now.

In a frying pan over medium heat, warm 1 tablespoon
of the oil. Add the sausage and fry, stirring occasionally,
until it begins to turn golden, about 3 minutes. Set aside.

In another frying pan, melt the butter over medium
heat. Add the apples and cook, stirring constantly, until
translucent, about 10 minutes. Set aside.

Shape the pizza dough and brush with the mustard.
Cover with the apples and sausage. Transfer the pizza to
the oven and bake for 10 minutes. Reduce the oven
temperature to 400°F (200°C) and bake until the crust
is golden, about 10 minutes. Drizzle the remaining
1 tablespoon oil over the top and serve immediately.

Serves 4

Prosciutto and Egg Pizza
PIZZA ALL' UOVO E PROSCIUTTO

cornmeal pizza dough (*recipe on page 13*)

¼ lb (120 g) prosciutto, thinly sliced

¼ lb (120 g) Fontina cheese, thinly sliced

4 eggs

4 large fresh plum (Roma) tomatoes, peeled and chopped, or canned plum tomatoes, drained and chopped

salt and freshly ground pepper

4 tablespoons (2 fl oz/60 ml) extra-virgin olive oil

An excellent dish to prepare for a special breakfast or brunch, although in Italy this pizza would just as likely be served as a casual one-course dinner. If you like, make it with your favorite cooked ham instead of the prosciutto.

Make the pizza dough. Preheat an oven to 450°F (220°C). If using a baking stone or tiles, place in the oven now.

Shape the pizza dough and cover with the prosciutto and Fontina. Transfer the pizza to the oven and bake for 10 minutes.

Remove the pizza from the oven and break the eggs over it, positioning each egg so that it rests in the center of a quarter wedge of the pizza. Cover with the tomatoes and season to taste with salt and pepper. Drizzle 3 tablespoons of the oil over the top. Quickly return the pizza to the oven, reduce the temperature to 400°F (200°C) and bake until the crust is golden, about 10 minutes. Drizzle with the remaining 1 tablespoon oil and serve immediately.

Serves 4

Curried Fruit and Cream Pizza
PIZZA DI FRUTTA AL CURRY

milk pizza dough *(recipe on page 13)*
⅓ cup (2 oz/60 g) raisins
2 apples, peeled, cored and cut into
    ½-inch (12-mm) dice
1 pear, peeled, cored and cut into
    ½-inch (12-mm) dice
1 slice pineapple, cored and cut into
    ½-inch (12-mm) dice
1 banana, peeled and cut into ½-inch
    (12-mm) dice
3 oz (90 g) seedless grapes
½ cup (4 fl oz/120 ml) heavy
    whipping (double) cream
2 tablespoons curry powder

A beguiling combination of sweetness and spice, this pizza makes an excellent accompaniment to foods cooked on a charcoal grill, such as chicken.

Make the pizza dough. Preheat an oven to 450°F (220°C). If using a baking stone or tiles, place in the oven now.

Place all the fruits in a saucepan. Pour in the cream and gently stir in the curry powder. Cover and cook over low heat until the fruits are soft and the cream is absorbed, about 15 minutes.

Roll out the pizza dough and cover with the fruit mixture. Transfer the pizza to the oven and bake for 10 minutes. Reduce the oven temperature to 400°F (200°C) and bake until the crust is golden, about 10 minutes. Serve immediately.

Serves 4

Gingered Pear Pizza

PIZZA ALLO ZENZERO

milk pizza dough (recipe on page 13)

4 Bosc pears, peeled, quartered and cored

½ cup (4 oz/120 g) sugar

2½ cups (20 fl oz/600 ml) good-quality red wine

3 tablespoons grated fresh ginger

The red wine in which the pears are simmered gives them a lovely ruby color, while its acidity helps to keep them firm. Make sure to form a rim high enough to contain the syrup. Apples make a fine substitute for the pears.

Make the pizza dough. Preheat an oven to 450°F (220°C). If using a baking stone or tiles, place in the oven now.

Place the pears in a saucepan and cover with the sugar, wine and ginger. Cook, uncovered, over low heat until soft, about 10 minutes. Transfer the pears with a slotted spoon to a bowl; set aside. Cook the wine mixture over low heat, stirring, until it is syrupy enough to coat the back of a spoon, about 20 minutes.

Roll out the pizza dough into one large pizza or 4 individual pizzas. Cover with the pears. Brush the pears with the wine syrup. Transfer to the oven and bake for 10 minutes. Reduce the oven temperature to 400°F (200°C) and bake until the crust is golden, about 10 minutes. Serve immediately.

Serves 4

Fresh Fruit Pizza
Pizza alla Frutta Fresca

milk pizza dough (recipe on page 13)
⅓ cup (2 oz/60 g) raisins
6 tablespoons (3 oz/90 g) sugar
2 tablespoons all-purpose (plain) flour
6 tablespoons (3 fl oz/90 ml) milk
2 eggs
1 tablespoon grated lemon zest
2 Golden or Red Delicious apples,
   peeled (optional), cored and sliced
2 Bosc pears, peeled (optional), cored
   and sliced
6 tablespoons (2 oz/60 g) pine nuts

Generous in its fresh fruit flavor and yet not too sweet, this pizza resembles a home-style tart. In summer, use fruits that are in abundance—peaches, nectarines, apricots, plums, cherries—in place of the apples and pears. Be sure to pinch up a fairly high rim on the pizza to contain the custard and any juices that run from the fruit during baking.

Make the pizza dough. Preheat an oven to 450°F (220°C). If using a baking stone or tiles, place in the oven now. In a small bowl soak the raisins in water to cover for 30 minutes.

In a mixing bowl vigorously stir the sugar and flour into the milk until fully dissolved. Add the eggs and whisk until well blended and a thick cream forms. Stir in the lemon zest.

Roll out the pizza dough and cover with the apple and pear slices, alternating them and arranging them in attractive patterns. Pour the egg mixture evenly over the top. Drain the raisins; scatter them and the pine nuts on top. Transfer the pizza to the oven and bake for 10 minutes. Reduce the oven temperature to 400°F (200°C) and bake until the crust is golden, about 10 minutes. Serve immediately.

Serves 4

Dried Fruit Pizza
Pizza alla Frutta Secca

½ cup (2 oz/60 g) dried apricots
⅓ cup (2 oz/60 g) prunes, pitted
⅓ cup (2 oz/60 g) raisins
⅓ cup (2 oz/60 g) dried peaches
1¼ cups (10 fl oz/300 ml) dessert
  wine
milk pizza dough (*recipe on page 13*)
⅓ cup (3 oz/90 g) sugar
⅓ cup (90 g) blanched almonds

The topping resembles an old-fashioned dried-fruit compote, making this a satisfying brunch or dessert pizza, or even an intriguing accompaniment to braised pork or beef. Port, Madeira or Vin Santo is an appropriate dessert wine for soaking the fruit. Substitute dried figs, if you like, for one of the fruits.

Place all the fruits together in a shallow bowl and add the wine to cover. Leave to soak for about 24 hours, occasionally stirring gently.

Make the pizza dough. Preheat an oven to 450°F (220°C). If using a baking stone or tiles, place in the oven now.

Drain the fruits, reserving the soaking liquid; set the fruits aside. Pour the liquid into a saucepan and add the sugar. Cook over low heat, stirring, until a syrup forms that is thick enough to coat the back of a spoon, about 10 minutes.

Roll out the pizza dough and cover with the drained fruits. Drizzle the wine syrup evenly over the top and decorate with the almonds. Transfer to the oven and bake for 10 minutes. Reduce the oven temperature to 400°F (200°C) and bake until the crust is golden, about 10 minutes. Serve immediately.

Serves 4

Banana and Ricotta Pizza with Ham

PIZZA DI BANANE E PROSCIUTTO COTTO

milk pizza dough (recipe on page 13)
¾ cup (7 oz/210 g) ricotta cheese
3 bananas, peeled and sliced
2 tablespoons unsalted butter, melted
3 oz (90 g) cooked ham, thinly sliced

Excellent sliced and served to guests at a special breakfast or brunch, this pizza can be made with crisply cooked and crumbled bacon instead of ham—or with no meat at all.

Make the pizza dough. Preheat an oven to 450°F (220°C). If using a baking stone or tiles, place in the oven now.

Roll out the pizza dough and spread the ricotta over it. Lay the banana slices on top in concentric circles. Brush the butter over the bananas. Transfer to the oven and bake for 10 minutes. Remove from the oven and cover with the ham slices. Quickly return to the oven, reduce the temperature to 400°F (200°C) and bake until the crust is golden, about 10 minutes. Serve immediately.

Serves 4

Mixed Berry Pizza
PIZZA ALLA FRUTTA DI BOSCO

milk pizza dough (recipe on page 13)

6 tablespoons (3 fl oz/90 ml) kirsch or
Grand Marnier

¾ cup plus 2 tablespoons (7 oz/210 g)
ricotta cheese

10 oz (300 g) mixed berries

6 tablespoons (3 oz/90 g) sugar

While supermarkets now make some berries available virtually year-round, this recipe will still be best in the warm months when berries—strawberries, raspberries, blueberries, black currants or some other local specialty—are at their seasonal best. Be sure to form a high rim to contain the juices; pinch the edge of the dough for a decorative touch.

Make the pizza dough. Preheat an oven to 450°F (220°C). If using a baking stone or tiles, place in the oven now.

In a small bowl stir the liqueur into the ricotta. Roll out the pizza dough and cover with the ricotta mixture. Top with the berries in an even layer. Sprinkle with the sugar. Transfer the pizza to the oven and bake for 10 minutes. Reduce the oven temperature to 400°F (200°C) and bake until the crust is golden, about 10 minutes. Serve immediately.

Serves 4

Coconut-Ricotta Cream Pizza
Pizza al Cocco

6 tablespoons (3 fl oz/90 ml)
   Frangelico or other sweet liqueur
6 tablespoons (1 oz/30 g) finely grated
   dried coconut
milk pizza dough (recipe on page 13)
1¼ cups (10 oz/300 g) ricotta cheese
6 tablespoons (3 oz/90 g) sugar

Reminiscent of an ultraelegant cheesecake, this pizza gains flavor, richness and texture from the combination of ricotta cheese, grated coconut and hazelnut-flavored Frangelico liqueur. Try substituting another favorite liqueur, if you like. For a special presentation, shape the pizza into an octagon with your hands.

In a small bowl stir together the Frangelico and coconut and let stand at room temperature for about 24 hours to soften the coconut.

Make the pizza dough. Preheat an oven to 450°F (220°C). If using a baking stone or tiles, place in the oven now.

Add the ricotta and sugar to the coconut mixture and stir vigorously until it has the consistency of thick cream. Roll out the pizza dough and cover with the coconut cream. Transfer the pizza to the oven and bake for 10 minutes. Reduce the oven temperature to 400°F (200°C) and bake until the crust is golden, about 10 minutes. Serve immediately.

Serves 4

Orange and Grand Marnier Pizza
PIZZA ALLE ARANCE AMARE

milk pizza dough *(recipe on page 13)*
½ cup (4 oz/120 g) sugar
½ cup (5 oz/155 g) orange marmalade
¼ cup (2 fl oz/60 ml) Grand Marnier
4 oranges, sliced crosswise about
   ¼ inch (6 mm) thick
9 strawberries, stemmed and sliced
   lengthwise, optional

Pretty enough to serve for dessert, this pizza is only slightly sweet, making it an ideal dish to offer guests at breakfast, brunch or lunch. It works just as well with apples or pears in place of the oranges.

Make the pizza dough. Preheat an oven to 450°F (220°C). If using a baking stone or tiles, place in the oven now.

Pour the sugar into a saucepan and melt it over low heat, without stirring. When the edges begin to turn gold, stir with a wooden spoon until the sugar turns gold and syrupy. Remove from the heat and add the marmalade, Grand Marnier and orange slices. Stir gently until the slices are well coated. Using tongs, pick up the slices, one at a time, and put them on a rack to drain. Reserve the syrup and keep hot.

Roll out the pizza dough and cover with the orange slices arranged in concentric circles. Transfer to the oven and bake for 10 minutes. Reduce the heat to 400°F (200°C) and bake until the crust is golden, about 10 minutes. Arrange the strawberry slices, if using, on top and drizzle with the hot syrup. Serve immediately.

Serves 4

Scallop Calzone
CALZONE CON LE CAPESANTE

12 sea scallops
juice of 3 lemons
freshly ground pepper
basic pizza dough *(recipe on page 10)*
4 tablespoons (2 fl oz/60 ml) extra-
  virgin olive oil
1 small onion, thinly sliced
1 fennel bulb, thinly sliced crosswise
2 tomatoes, peeled and chopped
1 tablespoon chopped fresh flat-leaf
  (Italian) parsley
salt

This recipe also works very well with fresh salmon, shrimp, crab meat or lobster.

Cut the scallops horizontally into slices ¼ inch (6 mm) thick, then cut in half vertically. Place in a shallow dish and pour in the lemon juice. Sprinkle with pepper and refrigerate, stirring occasionally, about 3 hours.

Make the pizza dough. Preheat an oven to 450°F (220°C). If using a baking stone or tiles, place in the oven now.

Warm 3 tablespoons of the oil in a frying pan over medium heat. Add the onion and sauté until golden, about 5 minutes. Add the fennel and tomatoes and cook, stirring, until the liquid evaporates, about 5 minutes. Add the parsley and season to taste with salt and pepper. Remove from the heat. Drain the scallops and mix into the pan.

Divide the pizza dough into 4 equal pieces. On a lightly floured board, shape each piece into a circle about 6 inches (15 cm) in diameter. Arrange one-fourth of the scallop mixture atop half of each circle, leaving a ½-inch (12-mm) border uncovered. Brush the edges of each circle with a little water and fold over the uncovered half to enclose the filling. Press the edges together to seal them. Transfer the calzone to the oven and bake for 10 minutes. Reduce the oven temperature to 400°F (200°C) and bake until the crust is golden, about 10 minutes. Drizzle the remaining 1 tablespoon oil over the tops and serve immediately.

Serves 4

Eggplant and Goat Cheese Calzone

CALZONE ALLE MELANZANE E FORMAGGIO DI CAPRA

herb pizza dough (*recipe on page 11*)
2 eggplants (aubergines), about 10 oz (300 g) total weight, thinly sliced crosswise
3 tablespoons extra-virgin olive oil
4 slices bacon
7 oz (210 g) fresh goat cheese
2 tablespoons minced fresh basil
salt and freshly ground pepper

If you like, this mixture is particularly delectable stuffed into miniature calzone no bigger than a baby's shoe.

Make the pizza dough. Preheat a broiler (griller). Preheat an oven to 450°F (220°C). If using a baking stone or tiles, place in the oven now.

Brush the eggplant slices on both sides with 1 tablespoon of the oil. Broil (grill) until tender, 2 minutes per side. Season with salt and pepper; set aside. Broil the bacon until crisp, 2 minutes per side. Drain on paper towels and crumble. In a small bowl crumble the cheese; stir in the basil and 1 tablespoon of the oil.

Divide the pizza dough into 4 equal pieces (or more for miniature calzone). On a lightly floured board, shape each piece into a circle. Arrange an equal amount of the eggplant atop half of each circle, leaving a small border uncovered. Sprinkle with the cheese and top with some bacon. Brush the edges of each circle with a little water and fold over the uncovered half to enclose the filling completely. Press the edges together to seal. Transfer the calzone to the oven and bake for 10 minutes. Reduce the temperature to 400°F (200°C) and bake until the crust is golden, about 10 minutes. Drizzle the remaining 1 tablespoon oil over the tops and serve immediately.

Serves 4

Ham and Apple Calzone
CALZONE AL PROSCIUTTO COTTO AFFUMICATO

potato pizza dough (recipe on
  page 12)
7 oz (210 g) smoked ham, coarsely
  chopped
2 Golden Delicious apples, peeled,
  cored and cut into ½-inch (12-mm)
  dice
½ cup (4 fl oz/120 ml) heavy
  whipping (double) cream
1 teaspoon freshly grated horseradish

In the Alto Adige region of northern Italy, where this home-style recipe originates, cooks sometimes use smoked pork loin in place of the ham. The addition of freshly grated horse-radish brings out the natural sweetness of the ham and apples. For a tantalizing presentation, bake the calzone seam-side up, then open for serving.

Make the pizza dough. Preheat an oven to 450°F (220°C). If using a baking stone or tiles, place in the oven now.

In a heavy-bottomed pot over low heat, combine the ham, apples, cream and horseradish. Cook, uncovered, stirring occasionally, until the apples are soft, about 5 minutes.

Divide the pizza dough into 4 equal pieces. On a lightly floured board, shape each piece into a circle about 6 inches (15 cm) in diameter. Arrange one-fourth of the apple-ham mixture atop half of each circle, leaving a ½-inch (12-mm) border uncovered. Brush the edges of each circle with a little water and fold over the uncovered half to enclose the filling completely. Press the edges together to seal them. Transfer the calzone to the oven and bake for 10 minutes. Reduce the oven temperature to 400°F (200°C) and bake until the crust is golden, about 10 minutes. Serve immediately.

Serves 4

Braised Pork Calzone
CALZONE DI MAIALE

herb pizza dough (recipe on page 11)
4 tablespoons (2 fl oz/60 ml) extra-
  virgin olive oil
1 small onion, thinly sliced
¾ lb (360 g) lean pork meat, cut into
  1-inch (2.5-cm) dice
1 red or yellow bell pepper
  (capsicum), seeded, deribbed and
  cut into ½-inch (12-mm) dice
½ cup (4 fl oz/120 ml) dry white wine
1 tablespoon dried oregano
salt and freshly ground pepper

The pork filling for this calzone is cooked in the Neapolitan style—braised in white wine with oregano. Cubes of boned lamb or chicken breast can be prepared in the same way.

Make the pizza dough. Preheat an oven to 450°F (220°C). If using a baking stone or tiles, place in the oven now.

Warm 3 tablespoons of the oil in a frying pan over medium heat. Add the onion and sauté, stirring continuously, until golden, about 5 minutes. Add the pork and bell pepper and continue to sauté until the pork takes on some color, about 10 minutes. Add the wine, sprinkle with the oregano and season to taste with salt and pepper. Cover and cook, stirring occasionally, until the wine evaporates, about 30 minutes.

Divide the pizza dough into 4 equal pieces. On a lightly floured board, shape each piece into a circle about 6 inches (15 cm) in diameter. Arrange one-fourth of the pork mixture atop half of each circle, leaving a ½-inch (12-mm) border uncovered. Brush the edges of each circle with a little water and fold over the uncovered half to enclose the filling completely. Press the edges together to seal them. Transfer the calzone to the oven to bake for 10 minutes. Reduce the oven temperature to 400°F (200°C) and bake until the crust is golden, about 10 minutes. Drizzle the remaining 1 tablespoon oil over the tops and serve immediately.

Serves 4

Braised Chicken Calzone
Calzone alla Cacciatora

basic pizza dough (recipe on page 10)

4 tablespoons (2 fl oz/60 ml) extra-virgin olive oil

1 small carrot, peeled and chopped

1 small onion, chopped

1 tablespoon minced fresh flat-leaf (Italian) parsley

½ chicken (about 2 lb/900 g), cut into 3 or 4 pieces

1¼ cups (10 fl oz/300 ml) good-quality red wine

10 oz (300 g) pearl onions

1 tablespoon juniper berries

1 tablespoon fresh thyme leaves

salt and freshly ground pepper

The chicken filling is cooked cacciatora, or "huntsman," style, braised with onions, wine and herbs. In Italy rabbit is a favorite meat and is often prepared this same way.

Make the pizza dough. Preheat an oven to 450°F (220°C). If using a baking stone or tiles, place in the oven now.

Warm 3 tablespoons of the oil in a heavy pan over low heat. Add the carrot, chopped onion and parsley; sauté until pale gold, about 10 minutes. Add the chicken, increase the heat and cook, stirring, until golden. Add the wine, pearl onions, juniper berries and thyme. Season with salt and pepper, reduce the heat, cover and cook until the juices evaporate and the chicken is tender, about 1 hour. Let cool, then remove the meat from the bones. Cut the meat into large pieces and return it to the pan. Mix well.

Divide the dough into 4 equal pieces. On a lightly floured board, shape each piece into a circle about 6 inches (15 cm) in diameter. Arrange one-fourth of the chicken mixture atop half of each circle, leaving a ½-inch (12-mm) border uncovered. Brush the edges of each circle with a little water and fold over the uncovered half to enclose the filling. Press the edges together to seal. Transfer the calzone to the oven and bake for 10 minutes. Reduce the temperature to 400°F (200°C) and bake until the crust is golden, about 10 minutes. Drizzle the remaining 1 tablespoon oil over the tops and serve immediately.

Serves 4

Two-Cheese and Garlic Calzone
CALZONE ALL'AGLIO E FONTINA

whole-wheat pizza dough (recipe on
   page 11)

4 tablespoons (2 fl oz/60 ml) extra-
   virgin olive oil

12 cloves garlic

6 oz (180 g) Gorgonzola cheese

1 tablespoon fresh lemon juice

6 oz (180 g) Fontina cheese, cut into
   pieces

*From northwestern Italy's Piedmont region, this aromatic
calzone is filled with sautéed garlic and Gorgonzola and
Fontina cheeses. Swiss cheese makes a good substitute for the
Fontina; instead of the Gorgonzola, you might try a creamy
Camembert or Brie pared of the white rind.*

Make the pizza dough. Preheat an oven to 450°F
(220°C). If using a baking stone or tiles, place in the
oven now.

Warm 3 tablespoons of the oil in a frying pan over low
heat. Add the garlic cloves and sauté until very soft and
golden, about 5 minutes. Remove from the heat.

In a mixing bowl combine the Gorgonzola and lemon
juice. Using a wooden spoon, work them together until
soft and smooth. Stir in the garlic and Fontina.

Divide the pizza dough into 4 equal pieces. On a lightly
floured board, shape each piece into a circle about 6
inches (15 cm) in diameter. Arrange one-fourth of the
garlic-cheese mixture atop half of each circle, leaving a
½-inch (12-mm) border uncovered. Brush the edges of
each circle with a little water and fold over the uncovered
half to enclose the filling. Press the edges together to seal
them. Transfer the calzone to the oven and bake for 10
minutes. Reduce the oven temperature to 400°F (200°C)
and bake until the crust is golden, about 10 minutes.
Drizzle the remaining 1 tablespoon oil over the tops and
serve immediately.

Serves 4

Spring Vegetable Calzone
CALZONE PRIMAVERA

basic pizza dough (recipe on page 10)
4 tablespoons (2 fl oz/60 ml) extra-
  virgin olive oil
1 onion, sliced
1 cup (4 oz/120 g) shelled green peas
¼ lb (120 g) green beans, cut into
  ½-inch (12-mm) pieces
1 carrot, peeled and cut into ½-inch
  (12-mm) pieces
¼ lb (120 g) trimmed asparagus tips,
  cut into ½-inch (12-mm) pieces
10 oz (300 g) canned plum (Roma)
  tomatoes, drained and chopped
salt and freshly ground pepper
1 tablespoon minced fresh flat-leaf
  (Italian) parsley

These crisp pockets of dough contain the finest harvest of the season. They are also delicious made with winter vegetables such as broccoli, fennel, Swiss chard (silverbeet) and cabbage.

Make the pizza dough. Preheat an oven to 450°F (220°C). If using a baking stone or tiles, place in the oven now.

  Warm 3 tablespoons of the oil in a frying pan over medium heat. Add the onion and sauté, stirring continuously, until golden, about 5 minutes. Add all the remaining vegetables and continue cooking until firm to the bite, about 5 minutes more. Season to taste with salt and pepper and mix in the parsley.

  Divide the pizza dough into 4 equal pieces. On a lightly floured board, shape each piece into a circle about 6 inches (15 cm) in diameter. Arrange one-fourth of the vegetable mixture atop half of each circle, leaving a ½-inch (12-mm) border uncovered. Brush the edges of each circle with a little water and fold over the uncovered half to enclose the filling completely. Press the edges together to seal them. Transfer the calzone to the oven and bake for 10 minutes. Reduce the oven temperature to 400°F (200°C) and bake until the crust is golden, about 10 minutes. Drizzle the remaining 1 tablespoon oil over the tops and serve immediately.

Serves 4

Fresh Tuna Calzone

CALZONE AL TONNO

herb pizza dough (recipe on page 11)
1 lemon
4 tablespoons (2 fl oz/60 ml) extra-
virgin olive oil
3 cloves garlic, chopped
1¼ lb (600 g) fresh tuna fillet, thinly
sliced against the grain
3 oz (90 g) Gaeta or Greek black
olives, pitted
salt and freshly ground pepper

Piquant Mediterranean flavors abound here: olive oil, garlic, lemon and black olives. Salmon or sole makes a good alternative to the tuna.

Make the pizza dough. Preheat an oven to 450°F (220°C). If using a baking stone or tiles, place in the oven now.

Grate the zest from the lemon and set aside. Remove all the white pith from the lemon, then thinly slice the lemon. Cut the slices into ½-inch (12-mm) pieces.

Warm 3 tablespoons of the oil in a frying pan over medium heat. Add the garlic and sauté, stirring continuously, until golden, about 5 minutes. Add the tuna, lemon pieces, lemon zest and olives. Cook for another 2 minutes. Season to taste with salt and pepper.

Divide the pizza dough into 4 equal pieces. On a lightly floured board, shape each piece into a circle about 6 inches (15 cm) in diameter. Arrange one-fourth of the tuna mixture atop half of each circle, leaving a ½-inch (12-mm) border uncovered. Brush the edges of each circle with a little water and fold over the uncovered half to enclose the filling completely. Press the edges together to seal them. Transfer the calzone to the oven and bake for 10 minutes. Reduce the oven temperature to 400°F (200°C) and bake until the crust is golden, about 10 minutes. Drizzle the remaining 1 tablespoon oil over the tops and serve immediately.

Serves 4

Sausage Calzone with Fennel Seeds

CALZONE ALLA SALSICCIA

whole-wheat pizza dough *(recipe on page 11)*

4 tablespoons (2 fl oz/60 ml) extra-virgin olive oil

3 cloves garlic, chopped

¾ lb (360 g) hot Neapolitan sausage, cut into slices ½-inch (12-mm) thick

1 tablespoon fennel seeds

2 tablespoons red wine vinegar

½ cup (4 fl oz/120 ml) good-quality red wine

This calzone features hot Neapolitan sausage, which mellows when it is cooked in red wine. Substitute any hot or sweet Italian sausage, or Spanish or Mexican chorizo.

Make the pizza dough. Preheat an oven to 450°F (220°C). If using a baking stone or tiles, place in the oven now.

Warm 3 tablespoons of the oil in a frying pan over medium heat. Add the garlic and sausage and sauté until the garlic begins to turn golden, about 5 minutes.

Add the fennel seeds and vinegar; cook until the vinegar evaporates, about 2 minutes. Add the wine, cover partially and cook until it evaporates, about 10 minutes.

Divide the pizza dough into 4 equal pieces. On a lightly floured board, shape each piece into a circle about 6 inches (15 cm) in diameter. Arrange one-fourth of the sausage mixture atop half of each circle, leaving a ½-inch (12-mm) border uncovered. Brush the edges of each circle with a little water and fold over the uncovered half to enclose the filling completely. Press the edges together to seal them. Transfer the calzone to the oven and bake for 10 minutes. Reduce the oven temperature to 400°F (200°C) and bake until the crust is golden, about 10 minutes. Drizzle the remaining 1 tablespoon oil over the tops and serve immediately.

Serves 4

Mussel and Clam Calzone
CALZONE AI FRUTTI DI MARE

basic pizza dough (recipe on page 10)
4 slices bacon
2 lb (900 g) clams in the shell,
   well scrubbed
2 lb (900 g) mussels in the shell,
   well scrubbed and beards removed
½ cup (4 fl oz/120 ml) dry white wine
1 tablespoon chopped fresh flat-leaf
   (Italian) parsley
3 shallots
3 tablespoons extra-virgin olive oil
1 tablespoon chopped fresh chives
salt and freshly ground pepper

Buy fresh shellfish with tightly closed shells, or shells that close when touched. Discard any that do not open upon cooking.

Make the dough. Preheat an oven to 450°F (220°C). If using a baking stone or tiles, place in the oven now.

In a frying pan, fry the bacon until crisp, about 5 minutes. Drain on paper towels and crumble.

Place the clams and mussels in a saucepan. Add the wine and parsley, cover and cook over medium heat until the shells open, a few minutes. Remove the meats and set aside. Strain the liquid into a small saucepan. Add the shallots. Reduce over low heat to 2 tablespoons, about 10 minutes. Strain the liquid into a bowl; whisk in 2 tablespoons of the oil. Mix in the clams, mussels, bacon and chives. Season to taste with salt and pepper.

Divide the pizza dough into 4 equal pieces. On a lightly floured board, shape each piece into a circle about 6 inches (15 cm) in diameter. Arrange one-fourth of the shellfish mixture atop half of each circle, leaving a ½-inch (12-mm) border uncovered. Brush the edges of each circle with a little water and fold over the uncovered half to enclose the filling completely. Press the edges together to seal them. Transfer the calzone to the oven and bake for 10 minutes. Reduce the oven temperature to 400°F (200°C) and bake until the crust is golden, about 10 minutes. Drizzle the remaining 1 tablespoon oil over the tops and serve immediately.

Serves 4

Glossary

The following glossary defines terms specifically as they relate to pizzas and pizza making. Included are major and unusual ingredients and basic techniques.

ANCHOVIES

Tiny saltwater fish, related to sardines; most often used as canned fillets that have been salted and preserved in oil. Imported anchovy fillets packed in olive oil are the most commonly available; those packed in salt, available canned in some Italian delicatessens, are considered the finest.

ASPARAGUS TIPS

The most tender 2–5 inches (5–13 cm) of the budding ends of asparagus stalks, prized for the delicacy of their flavor and texture.

BAKING POWDER

Commercial baking product combining three ingredients: baking soda, the source of the carbon-dioxide gas that causes quick batters and doughs to rise; an acid, such as cream of tartar, calcium acid phosphate or sodium aluminum sulphate, which, when the powder is combined with a liquid, causes the baking soda to release its gas; and a starch such as cornstarch or flour, to keep the powder from absorbing moisture.

BASIL

Sweet, spicy herb popular in Italian and French cooking, particularly as a seasoning for tomatoes and tomato sauces.

BELGIAN ENDIVE

Leaf vegetable with refreshing, slightly bitter spear-shaped leaves, white to pale yellow-green—or sometimes red—in color, tightly packed in cylindrical heads 4–6 inches (10–15 cm) long. Also known as chicory and witloof.

BREAD CRUMBS

For authentic Italian-style bread crumbs, choose a good-quality, rustic-style loaf made of unbleached wheat flour, with a firm, coarse-textured crumb; usually sold in bakeries as country-style, rustic or peasant bread. For fresh crumbs, cut away the crusts from the fresh bread and crumble the crumb by hand or in a blender or food processor fitted with the metal blade. For dry crumbs, place slices of bread on a baking pan and dry slowly in an oven set at its lowest temperature, then process in a blender or food processor.

CAPERS

Small, pickled buds of a bush common to the Mediterranean, used whole as a savory flavoring or garnish.

CHILI PEPPERS

Any of a wide variety of peppers prized for the mild-to-hot spiciness they impart as a seasoning. Red, ripe chilies are sold fresh and dried. Fresh green chilies include the mild-to-hot, dark green poblano; the long, mild Anaheim; and the small, fiery jalapeño. When handling any chili, wear kitchen gloves to prevent any cuts or abrasions on your hands from contacting the pepper's volatile oils. Wash your hands well with warm, soapy water, and take special care not to touch your eyes or any other sensitive areas.

CHIVES

Mild, sweet herb with a flavor reminiscent of onion, to which it is related. Although available dried in the herb-and-spice section of a supermarket, fresh chives possess the best flavor.

CLAMS

Bivalve mollusks prized for their sweet, tender flesh. Sold live in their shells, or sometimes already shucked, in good-quality fish markets or supermarket seafood departments.

CORNMEAL

Granular flour, ground from the dried kernels of yellow or white corn, with a sweet, robust flavor;

BELL PEPPER

Fresh, sweet-fleshed, bell-shaped member of the pepper family; also known as a capsicum. Most common in the unripe green form; ripened red or yellow varieties are also available. Creamy pale-yellow, orange and purple-black types may also be found.

To prepare a raw bell pepper, cut it in half lengthwise with a sharp knife. Pull out the stem section from each half, along with the cluster of seeds attached to it.

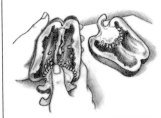

Remove any remaining seeds, along with any thin white membranes, or ribs, to which they are attached.

Cut the pepper halves into quarters, strips or thin slices, as called for in the specific recipe.

When a recipe calls for roasted bell peppers, place the whole peppers on a baking sheet. Roast in a 400°F (200°C) oven, under a broiler (griller) or atop a grill, turning occasionally, until their skin is evenly blackened. Cover with a cotton towel and, as soon as they are cool enough to handle, use your fingers to peel off the blackened skins and to remove the stems, seeds and ribs. Then tear or cut the peppers as directed in the recipe.

DRIED FRUIT
Intensely flavored and satisfyingly chewy, many forms of sun-dried or kiln-dried fruit may be used as toppings for dessert pizzas. Usually found in specialty-food stores or supermarket baking sections. Some of the most popular options include:

Raisins
Variety of dried grapes, popular as a snack on their own. Use seedless dark raisins or golden raisins (sultanas).

Apricots
Pitted whole or halved fruit (below, right), sweet and slightly tangy.

Prunes
Variety of dried plum (above, left), with a rich-tasting, dark, fairly moist flesh.

Peaches
Halved or quartered, pitted and flattened fruit; sweet and slightly tangy.

---

sometimes used to enhance pizza dough. Commercial cornmeal, sold in supermarkets, lacks the kernel's husk and germ and is available in fine or coarser grinds. Stone-ground cornmeal, made from whole corn kernels, produces a richer flour.

CREAM, HEAVY WHIPPING
Cream with a high butterfat content—at least 36 percent. Also called double cream.

CURRY POWDER
Generic term for blends of spices commonly used to flavor Indian-style dishes. Most curry powders will include coriander, cumin, chili, fenugreek and turmeric; other additions may include cardamom, cinnamon, cloves, allspice, **fennel** seeds and **ginger.**

EGGPLANT
Vegetable-fruits, also known as aubergines, with tender, mildly earthy, sweet flesh. Their shiny skins vary in color from purple to red and from yellow to white, and their shapes range from small and round or oval to long and slender to large and pear shaped. The most common variety is large, purple and globular; but slender, purple Asian eggplants, more tender and with fewer, smaller seeds, are available with increasing frequency in markets.

FENNEL
Crisp, refreshing, mildly anise-flavored bulb vegetable, also known by its Italian name, *finocchio*. Fine, feathery leaves, which rise from the center of the bulb on narrow tubular stems, are used as a fresh or dried herb. The crescent-shaped seeds are dried and used as a spice.

FLOUR, ALL-PURPOSE
The most common flour for making pizza dough, this bleached and blended (hard and soft wheats) variety is available in all supermarkets. Also called plain flour.

FLOUR, WHOLE-WHEAT
Pale brown flour derived from whole, unbleached wheat berries, from which neither the bran nor the germ has been removed. Also known as wholemeal flour.

FONTINA
Firm, creamy, mild-tasting Italian cheese made from sheep's milk.

FRANGELICO
Italian sweet liqueur based on wild hazelnuts and herbs.

GARLIC
Pungent bulb popular worldwide as a flavoring ingredient, both raw and cooked. For the best

flavor, purchase whole heads of garlic, separating individual cloves from the head as needed; do not purchase more than one head at a time, as garlic can shrivel and lose its flavor with prolonged storage. To peel a garlic clove, place on a work surface and cover with the side of a large chef's knife. Press down firmly but carefully on the side of the knife to crush the clove slightly. The dry skin will then slip off easily.

GINGER
The rhizome of the tropical ginger plant, which yields a sweet, strong-flavored spice. The whole rhizome may be purchased fresh in a supermarket or vegetable market. Ginger pieces may be found crystallized or candied in specialty-food shops or supermarket baking sections, or preserved in syrup in specialty shops or Asian food sections. Dried and ground ginger is commonly available in jars or tins in the spice section.

GOAT CHEESE, FRESH
Fresh and creamy cheese, with a distinctively sharp tang. Fresh goat cheeses are sold shaped into small rounds, about 2 inches (5 cm) in diameter, or logs 1–2 inches (2.5–5 cm) in diameter and 4–6 inches (10–15 cm) long. Some are coated with mixtures of herbs, with pepper, or with ash. Also known as *chèvre.*

GORGONZOLA
Italian variety of tangy, creamy, blue-veined cheese.

GRAND MARNIER
A popular commercial brand of orange-flavored liqueur, distinguished by its pure Cognac base.

HORSERADISH
Pungent, hot-tasting root; a member of the mustard family, sold fresh and whole, already grated and bottled, or in dry granulated forms.

JUNIPER BERRIES
Aromatic, small dried berries of the juniper tree. Available in the supermarket spice section or in specialty-food shops.

KIRSCH
Dry, clear brandy distilled from black morello cherries and infused with their unique aroma and taste. Do not confuse with crème de kirsch, a sweet cherry liqueur.

MADEIRA
Sweet, amber-colored dessert wine originating in the Portuguese island of Madeira.

MARJORAM
Pungent, aromatic herb used dried or fresh to season meats (particularly lamb), poultry, seafood, vegetables and eggs.

MOZZARELLA

Rindless white, mild-tasting Italian variety of cheese traditionally made from water buffalo's milk and sold fresh. Commercially produced and packaged cow's milk mozzarella is now much more common, although it has less flavor.

MUSSELS

Before cooking, the popular, bluish black–shelled bivalves require special cleaning to remove any dirt adhering to their shells and to remove their "beards," the fibrous threads by which the mussels connect to

OLIVES, BLACK

Throughout Mediterranean Europe, black olives are cured in combinations of salt, seasonings, brines, vinegars and oils to produce pungently flavored results. Good-quality cured olives, such as Gaeta or Greek varieties, are available in ethnic delicatessens, specialty-food shops and well-stocked supermarkets.

To pit an olive, use a special olive pitter, which grips it and pushes out the pit in one squeeze. Or carefully slit the olive lengthwise down to the pit with a small, sharp knife. Pry the flesh away from the pit; if the flesh sticks to the pit, carefully cut it away.

rocks or piers in the coastal waters where they live. Rinse the mussels thoroughly under running cold water. One at a time, hold them under the water and scrub with a firm-bristled brush to remove any stubborn dirt. Firmly grasp the fibrous beard attached to the side of each mussel and pull it off. Check all the mussels carefully, discarding those whose shells are not tightly closed.

NUTMEG

Popular baking spice that is the hard pit of the fruit of the nutmeg tree. May be bought already ground or, preferably, whole, to be freshly ground as needed with any fine grater or a special nutmeg grater or grinder.

OLIVE OIL

Extra-virgin olive oil, extracted from olives on the first pressing without use of heat or chemicals, is preferred for pizza making. Be sure to choose an oil labeled "extra-virgin." Many brands, varying in color and strength of flavor, are now available; choose one that suits your taste. The higher-priced extra-virgin olive oils usually are of better quality. Store in an airtight container away from heat and light.

OREGANO

Aromatic, pungent and spicy Mediterranean herb—also known as wild marjoram—used fresh or dried as a seasoning for all kinds of savory dishes.

PANCETTA

Italian-style unsmoked bacon cured with salt and pepper. May be sold flat or rolled into a large sausage shape. Available in Italian delicatessens and specialty-food stores.

PAPRIKA

Powdered spice derived from the dried paprika pepper; popular in several European cuisines and available in sweet, mild and hot forms. Hungarian paprika is the best, but Spanish paprika, which is mild, may also be used. Buy in small quantities from shops with a high turnover, to ensure a fresh, flavorful supply.

PARMESAN

Hard, thick-crusted Italian cow's milk cheese with a sharp, salty, full flavor resulting from at least two years of aging. Buy in block form, to grate or shave fresh. The finest Italian variety is designated parmigiano-reggiano.

PARSLEY, FLAT-LEAF

Variety of the popular fresh herb with broad, flat leaves that have a more pronounced flavor than the common crinkly-leafed type. Also called Italian parsley.

PEAR, BOSC

Long, slender, tapered variety of autumn-to-winter pear with yellow-and-russet skin and slightly grainy, solid-textured white flesh with a hint of acidity. A good cooking pear.

PINE NUTS

Small, ivory-colored seeds extracted from the cones of a

species of pine tree, with a rich, slightly resinous flavor. Also known by the Italian *pinoli*.

PROSCIUTTO

Italian raw ham, a specialty of Parma, cured by dry-salting for one month, followed by air-drying in cool curing sheds for half a year or longer. Usually cut into tissue-thin slices, the better to appreciate its intense flavor and deep pink color.

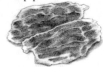

RADICCHIO

Vegetable whose leaves are reddish purple and ivory or green and have a mildly bitter flavor. Also known as red chicory.

RICOTTA

Very light, bland Italian cheese made with twice-cooked milk—traditionally sheep's milk, although cow's milk ricotta is far more common. Made from the whey left over from making other cheeses, commonly **mozzarella** and provolone.

ROMANO

Italian variety of cheese traditionally made from sheep's milk, now made from goat and cow's milk as well. Sold either fresh or, more commonly, aged. The aged form is similar to but notably more tangy than **Parmesan.** Buy in block form, to shave or grate as needed.

ROSEMARY

Mediterranean herb, used either fresh or dried, with a strong aromatic flavor well suited to lamb and veal, as well as poultry, seafood and vegetables.

SAGE

Pungent herb, used either fresh or dried, that goes particularly well with fresh or cured pork, lamb, veal or poultry.

SALMON, SMOKED

Purchase smoked salmon freshly sliced from a good-quality delicatessen. Lox, which is a salt-cured salmon, and Nova, which is a cold-smoked salmon, are commonly sold in Jewish delicatessens; they have oilier textures and in most cases are not acceptable substitutes for smoked salmon.

SAUSAGE, ITALIAN

Fresh Italian sausage is generally made from ground pork, seasoned with salt, pepper and spices. Those made in the style of northern Italy are usually sweet and mild, sometimes flavored with **fennel** seed. Southern-style sausages, such as Neapolitan varieties, tend to be hotter, often flavored with flakes of dried **chili pepper.**

SCALLOPS

Bivalve mollusks that come in two common varieties: the round flesh of sea scallops is usually 1½ inches (4 cm) in diameter, while the bay scallop is considerably smaller. Usually sold already shelled.

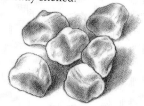

SESAME SEEDS

Tiny, pale ivory-colored seeds with a mild, nutty flavor; used most often as a garnish.

SHALLOT

Small member of the onion family with brown skin, white-to-purple flesh and a flavor resembling a cross between sweet onion and **garlic.**

SWISS CHEESE

Firm whole-milk cheese, pale yellow in color, with distinctive holes that grow larger and more numerous with ripening.

THYME

Fragrant, clean-tasting, small-leaved herb popular fresh or dried as a seasoning for poultry, light meats, seafood or vegetables.

TROUT, SMOKED

Sold in specialty-food stores and delicatessens, either in fillets or as whole fish requiring skinning and boning, smoked trout has a mild, sweet flavor and moist, tender texture.

VIN SANTO

Intense Tuscan dessert wine made from grapes partially dried away from direct sunlight for a couple of months before pressing, then aged in oak for four to five years.

VINEGAR, RED WINE

Literally "sour" wine, vinegar results when certain strains of yeast cause wine—or some other alcoholic liquid—to ferment for a second time, turning it acidic. The best-quality wine vinegars begin with good-quality wine. Red wine vinegar, like the wine from which it is made, has a more robust flavor than vinegar produced from white wine.

YEAST, ACTIVE DRY

One of the most widely available forms of yeast for baking, commonly sold in individual

TOMATOES

Except in July, August and September, when sun-ripened tomatoes are available, canned Italian tomatoes are far superior to any hothouse variety for cooking purposes. In either case, use plum tomatoes, sometimes called egg or Roma tomatoes, as they have the best texture.

To peel fresh tomatoes, follow these simple steps:

Bring a saucepan filled with water to a boil. Using a small, sharp knife, cut out the core from the stem end of the tomato. Then cut a shallow X in the skin at the tomato's base.

Submerge for about 20 seconds in boiling water, then remove and dip in a bowl of cold water.

Starting at the X, peel the skin from the tomato.

Cut the tomatoes in half and turn each half cut-side down. Cut as directed in recipe.

To seed a tomato, cut it in half crosswise. Squeeze gently to force out the seed sacks.

packages containing a scant 1 tablespoon (¼ oz/7 g) and found in the baking section of the supermarket. Seek out one of the new strains of fast-acting yeast available in specialty-food stores. If using fresh cake yeast, substitute ½ oz (15 g) for 1 tablespoon active dry yeast.

ZEST

Thin, brightly colored, outermost layer of a citrus fruit's peel, containing most of its aromatic essential oils—a lively source of flavor in baking.

ZUCCHINI

Slender, tube-shaped relative of the squash, also referred to as summer squash or courgette, with edible green, yellow or green-and-cream–striped skin and pale, tender flesh. Smaller-sized squash have a finer texture and flavor, and less pronounced seeds, than those that have been grown larger.

Index

ACKNOWLEDGMENTS

The publishers would like to thank the following people and organizations for their generous assistance and support in producing this book:
Michael and Anthony Dunkley, Amy Morton, Ken DellaPenta, Sharon-Ann C. Lott, Stephen W. Griswold, the buyers for Gardener's Eden, and the buyers and store managers for Pottery Barn and Williams-Sonoma stores.

The following kindly lent props for the photography: Biordi Art Imports, Fillamento, Galisteo, Stephanie Greenleigh, Philippe Henry de Tessan, Sue Fisher King, Karen Nicks, Lorraine & Judson Puckett, Gianfranco Savio, Sue White and Chuck Williams.

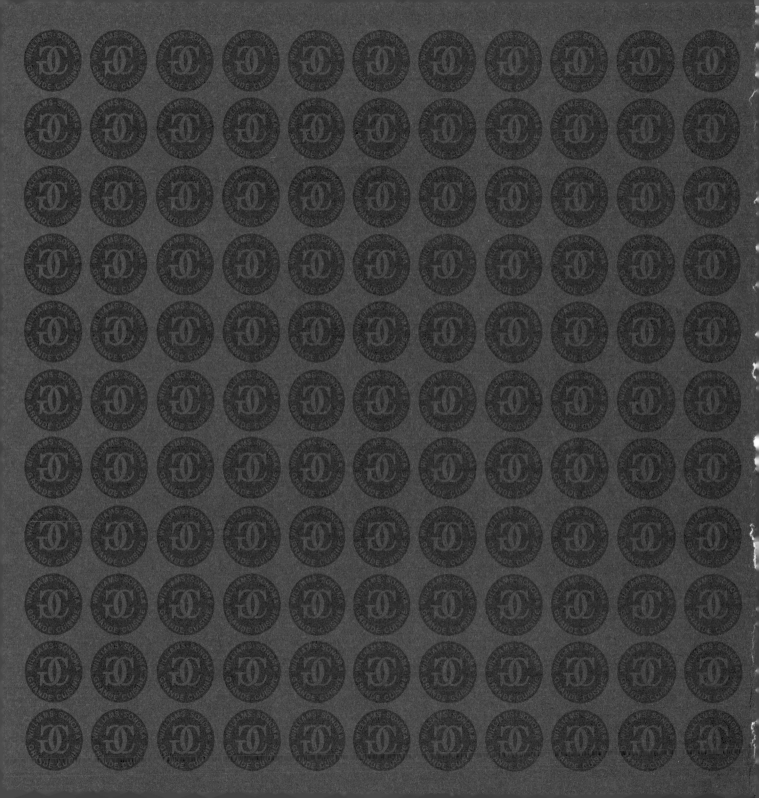